Nurturing CREATIVITY

An Essential Mindset for Young Children's Learning

Rebecca Isbell &
Sonia Akiko Yoshizawa

National Association for the Education of Young Children
Washington, DC

naeyc®

National Association for the
Education of Young Children
1313 L Street NW, Suite 500
Washington, DC 20005-4101
202-232-8777 • 800-424-2460
www.naeyc.org

NAEYC Books

Senior Director, Content Strategy
and Development
Susan Friedman

Editor-in-Chief
Kathy Charner

Senior Creative Design Manager
Audra Meckstroth

Managing Editor
Mary Jaffe

Senior Editor
Holly Bohart

Senior Creative Design Specialist
Lindsay Dirienzo

Associate Editor
Rossella Procopio

Through its publications program,
the National Association for the
Education of Young Children
(NAEYC) provides a forum for
discussion of major issues and ideas
in the early childhood field, with
the hope of provoking thought and
promoting professional growth. The
views expressed or implied in this
book are not necessarily those of the
Association.

In all instances, the names of the children and teachers
pictured or described in this book have been changed to
protect confidentiality.

Photo Credits

Courtesy of Ann Marie Cornelison: 35–36 (all), 130 (right), 133
(bottom right), and 134 (top and middle)

Courtesy of Edwel Granadozo: introduction photo, 15 (top), 22,
29, 40, 50, 53, 60–62 (all), 117, 118, 120 (top left), 122 (all), 127,
144 (top left, center, and right; bottom left and center), and 147

Courtesy of Jenifer Lingerfelt: 42 (both), 55 (all), 71 (both),
and 75

Courtesy of Hillary Schimd: 54 and 103 (top left, center,
and right)

Courtesy of Abby Williams and Beth Culhane: 110 (all)

Copyright © NAEYC: 89

Copyright © iStock: 44, 77, 98, 109 (all), 111–113 (all), 132 (top
left and right), 137, and 149

All other photos are courtesy of Sonia Akiko Yoshizawa

Library of Congress Control Number: 2016947630

ISBN: 978-1-938113-21-5

Item 1129

Contents

Chapter 3: The Environment: A Look Inside Classrooms That Inspire Creativity

Chapter 4: Characteristics of Creative Children and Adults 63

Chapter 8: Displaying and Documenting Children's Work   123

Chapter 9: Expanding the Community of Support

Epilogue

References

About the Authors

Acknowledgments

Alex (age 4) discovers the joy of painting on a big canvas as he explores several different ways of moving his paintbrush. His strokes go from side to side, then up and down. "Look, I can p[...] higher!" He jumps up high and splashes the paint on the canv[...] with his paintbrush. After several jumps, the red paint drops [...] his face as well. He giggles.

Introduction

A little confidence in creativity leads to a lot of confidence in everything else.

—David Kelley, *Creative Confidence: Unleashing the Creative Potential Within Us All*

During the early years, young children are continually demonstrating their amazing creative abilities (Kelley & Kelley 2013). Throughout their day, they form new, never-before-heard words, design towering structures as symbols of their world, compose musical lyrics to accompany their activities, create fanciful stories where they decide what happens, and solve challenging problems. This is a grand period for young creative thinkers! But can they maintain this amazing creative thinking throughout their lifetime? As adults, they will need to be innovative in their work environment and become creative collaborators who can solve global problems; however, between the early years and adulthood, many children become less confident in their creative abilities and more hesitant to try new things (Kelley & Kelley 2013). During this journey, will they find a passion that will nurture their creative thinking? Let us investigate together how we can nurture young children's *creative confidence* so they can maintain these remarkable abilities now and throughout their lives.

Creative confidence is believing in your ability to influence the world around you. It is a conviction that you can achieve what you set out to do (Kelley & Kelley 2013).

Csikszentmihalyi (2014), a renowned expert on creativity, notes, "It is easier to enhance creativity by changing conditions in the environment than by trying to make people think more creatively" (1). If an environment is designed to nurture young children's creativity, support their efforts, and provide opportunities that will challenge their thinking, it is possible to build the creative confidence that will assist them through the sometimes frustrating process of creating and problem solving. When children feel inspired by a supportive environment and encouraged for their unique ideas, they learn to believe in their own abilities and are more likely to continue to act on and refine their ideas.

Early childhood teachers have the amazing opportunity to value, support, and design an environment that nurtures young children's creative abilities, a place where children are able to think, explore, play with ideas, and be courageous in their innovations. In this captivating environment, they find personally interesting projects, have opportunities to collaborate with others, and explore new possibilities. Throughout this book, we provide stories and examples of ways to support children's creative thinking in different areas of the classroom and across many learning domains. This book celebrates teachers who strive to provide opportunities for young children to thrive and offer experiences that build on children's strengths.

Overview

In this book, we

> Examine the creative process as it relates to young children—particularly in preschool, pre-K, and kindergarten—and teachers

> Investigate the thinking of theorists and creative thinkers

> Observe children's creative work

> Identify how teachers can model and inspire creativity while enriching and expanding their own

> Examine intriguing experiences that challenge young children to think in new and different ways

> Investigate how teachers can build an environment that nurtures young children's creativity and considers their holistic development

In addition, we explain and illustrate the teacher's essential role in supporting children's creativity—including designing the environment and activities, valuing children's ideas and efforts, questioning to help children go deeper, providing provocation to stimulate ideas and exploration, collaborating with children, and pulling back to encourage independence. Throughout the book, sections titled "Reflections" prompt teachers to think about practices related to creativity and to help you apply these ideas to your own classroom environment.

The arts—including the visual arts, music making, drama/storytelling, and movement/dance—are often considered an effective way to inspire children's creative thinking. Creativity is connected less often with science, math, reading, technology, social studies, and other curriculum areas; however, children express creativity in *all* domains, and these areas offer tremendous opportunities for creative planning, discovery, experimentation, and problem solving. Offering children engaging learning opportunities in a variety of domains will help them find their interests, investigate new areas, identify personal passions, and extend their thinking.

Each chapter ends with a section titled "Evidence of Creating, Thinking, and Learning," which includes colorful visuals, children's writing, their creations, and stories of remarkable creative work by young children. Each section provides inspirational examples of children's creative work that can be shared with families, peers, supervisors, and administrators. These projects provide concrete documentation that reveals how young children think while exploring a science concept, painting murals, constructing a mathematical pattern, writing plays, improvising music, participating in socio-dramatic play, collaborating in decision making, and engaging in problem solving. The examples of colorful photographs, indoor and outdoor paintings, interesting lighting effects, music compositions, sensory materials, original plays, and science projects may inspire you to explore these options and others with the children you teach.

The goals for this book are to

> Help teachers recognize the importance of nurturing and supporting children's creative thinking

> Establish creative thinking as an essential component in every early childhood classroom

> Inspire teachers working with young children to select materials and design their classroom environment in ways that will nurture the creative process

> Encourage teachers and children to play with ideas, materials, humor, and imagination to expand the possibilities for creativity

> Illustrate how the arts can provide an avenue to ignite creativity and creative thinking in all areas of the curriculum and daily life

> Provide examples of amazing creations by young children that provide essential evidence of their creative thinking

> Build on the wonderful things that are happening in many early childhood classrooms that nurture the creativity of all young children

> Expand teachers' understanding that creativity can happen in many different places throughout the day and in various areas of learning

> Help teachers celebrate their own creativity and use their ideas to inspire children to reach their creative potential

A Plan for Creative Action: Reflection

As you read this book, use the following questions to guide your thinking:

> How can I support young children's creative development?

> How can I design my classroom environment so it nurtures children's creative confidence?

> How can I give children the encouragement they need to inspire their creativity?

> How can I expand my thinking and approaches to include more creative opportunities for children?

To help children reach their full potential, it is important to design and implement environments that nurture their creativity while preparing them to be successful today and in the future. This book is designed to provide a variety of people who work with young children, including early childhood teachers, program administrators, and teachers in training, with the spark and invigoration needed to nurture young creative minds.

Chapter 1

What Is Creative Thinking and Why Do We Need It Now?

Creativity is the greatest gift of human intelligence. The more complex the world becomes, the more creative we need to be to meet its challenges.

—Ken Robinson, *Out of Our Minds: Learning to be Creative*

Mitchel Resnick, director at the Massachusetts Institute of Technology (MIT) Media Laboratory, named his research group Lifelong Kindergarten because he was inspired by what he observed in the kindergartens he visited. He described these classrooms as filled with children exploring, experimenting, designing, and creating things in collaboration with each other. He saw two young children building with wooden blocks, and over time these blocks became a collection of towers. Other children participated in the play and contributed novel ideas, such as readjusting the space between towers to maneuver toy vehicles, constructing towers of various sizes, and building wider foundations (Resnick 2007).

> In this book, creativity refers to children actively producing ideas, inventing or making something for the first time, or coming up with unique and different ways of expressing their thinking.

The creative thinking that Resnick observed in these kindergartens—and that he hoped would infuse his research group—demonstrates how young children can imagine what they wish to do, create a project based on their ideas, and play with or use their creations. These children were trying new ideas and taking risks. They talked and listened to each other and reflected on their experiences, which generated new ideas. However, Resnick (2007) expresses concern that programs are moving toward more teacher-directed activities with an academic focus and limiting opportunities for children to identify and problem-solve on projects of their own interest. Like Resnick and many in the early childhood field, we believe that there is an urgent need for educators to encourage children's independent, creative thinking in preschool, pre-K, and kindergarten.

What Is Creativity?

Definitions of creativity are as varied as the people who write them. Carson (2010) and Isenberg and Durham (2015) define creativity as having an idea that is unique or original, and also useful or adaptable. For example, when a teacher adds fabrics with a variety of textures, colors, and sizes to the dramatic play area so children can create their own costumes, she is supporting their creative thinking and nurturing their unique, adaptable ideas. Others describe creativity as seeing possibilities, making things happen, making connections between things that do not seem to be related, and coming up with solutions to problems for which there is no single right answer (Isenberg & Jalongo 2014; Starko 2014). Creativity may also be defined and organized as terms for identifying problems and forming solutions, including **fluency** (generating many ideas), **flexibility** (the ability to move from one idea to another), **elaboration** (using an existing idea and extending it), and **originality** (forming unique possibilities) (Fox & Schirrmacher 2015; Torrance 1965).

In this book, creativity refers to children actively producing ideas, inventing or making something for the first time, or coming up with unique and different ways of expressing their thinking. A creative act is one that is meaningful for the child.

How do we study creativity? Keith Sawyer (2012), a leading researcher in creativity, innovation, and learning, and the author of *Explaining Creativity: The Science of Human Innovation*, describes three types of research studies on creativity:

Nurturing Creativity: An Essential Mindset for Young Children's Learning

- The **individualistic approach**: looking at individuals who show creativity, such as taking a different path to drive to the same destination or making a particular recipe differently each time

- The **cognitive approach**: focusing on mental processes that occur when people are engaged in creative behavior, such as a choreographer who is actively engaged in thinking, creating, improvising, revising, and remembering dance moves to accompany a song

- The **social-cultural approach**: focusing on creative people working together in social and cultural systems, such as jazz ensembles or product improvement teams

Rather than continuing to study these aspects in isolation, Sawyer suggests using the **interdisciplinary approach**, which combines all three approaches to explain creativity.

Tania's Story

How do you recognize a child's creativity? Tania, a curious, active 4-year-old, enjoys exploring and generating unusual ideas. One day, her teacher brings in a stack of cardboard packaging pieces. She adds these novel pieces to the art center to stimulate children's creative thinking. Tania picks up the pieces to investigate their size, shape, and texture. She is particularly interested in the large round hole in the center of each piece of cardboard. She takes one of the cardboard pieces and brings it to the table. She sits and looks at the cardboard. Then, she goes back to get a second piece, returns to the table, and looks intently at both pieces. After several minutes, she returns to select a third piece to add to her collection. She looks, manipulates, and thinks for an extended period of time. An observer might wonder whether she is being productive. She hasn't produced anything or communicated any ideas.

Finally, Tania stands up and begins to collect other materials. She gets glue, a pencil, and several sheets of small tissue paper in an assortment of colors that are stored in the area. First, she glues a piece of blue tissue paper over the hole of one cardboard piece. Next, she glues pink tissue paper on another piece, and finally, she covers the hole of the last piece of cardboard with yellow tissue paper. She positions the three cardboard pieces by standing them up on their edges and glues them together, forming a three-dimensional structure. She looks for string or yarn but cannot find any, so she asks her teacher for some help.

Returning to the table, she punches a hole in the top of each cardboard piece and strings the yarn through the holes. She picks up her creation and takes it to her teacher. "Would you please hang this in the window? When the sun shines and it turns, it will make a rainbow!"

Story Reflection

This story helps identify Tania as an independent thinker who comes up with ideas and implements them on her own. Like many young children, she is inquisitive and energetic. She wants to explore and investigate unusual concrete materials, which she later uses to represent her ideas. She is inspired when she makes the connection between the holes in the cardboard pieces and the easily accessible colored tissue papers. Her creative ideas become visible when she attaches the three-dimensional pieces together and makes them into a rainbow mobile. Tania's teacher collects unusual materials that she thinks will inspire children to think in new ways. She displays the materials to invite exploration and encourage engagement that could stimulate children's thinking. She gives Tania the freedom to investigate without interrupting or asking intrusive questions and lets her manipulate the materials to come up with her own artistic design. Once Tania is satisfied with her composition, the teacher supports her efforts by hanging her mobile in a window that receives the morning sun and accentuates the bright colors she used.

The Early Years of Creative Learning

Some believe that creativity is not a trait that a baby is born with but rather a part of development and learning that occurs over time. Unless creativity is supported, encouraged, and nurtured, it is unlikely that a child will reach his or her full creative potential (Bruce 2011). Bruce explains that infants and toddlers show evidence of emergent creativity very early in life. For instance, when a parent engages her baby with *parentese*—high-pitched, singsong speech along with simple sentences and exaggerated facial expressions—the infant plays with language as part of the verbal interaction. Vygotsky ([1930–35] 1978) suggests that the highest form of thinking occurs in the context of this kind of social relationship. When the baby and adult interact, each is discovering how to be creative and thoughtful.

As children grow and reach toddlerhood, they may test the limits of adults as they try to establish their autonomy. This is an important aspect of development as they explore their environment and discover how to influence their world. During the toddler and preschool years, children begin to recognize and establish themselves as separate from others in their environment. At the same time, they still need to feel that they belong to the group and are accepted by their peers and adults. This emotionally safe and secure place with supportive adults allows young children to be creative and venture into new experiences.

We believe that the preschool years are a highly creative period—perhaps one of the most creative periods of human development. Young children express creativity in different ways, and their environment should be responsive to their individual abilities in ways that inspire creative feelings and ideas (Tegano, Moran, & Sawyers 1991). This is a reciprocal relationship in which the child influences the environment and the environment, in turn, affects the young child.

Why Is Creative Thinking So Critical?

Today's children will likely grow up to live in a world very different from that of the present, working in careers that do not yet exist, using methods and technologies that have not yet been invented, and valuing commodities that have not yet been created (Trilling & Fadel 2009). To succeed and thrive in that world, children will need new ways of thinking and new skill sets. This new world will need children and adults who can think creatively to find innovative solutions to problems.

Expanding Information and Technology

Every day the amount of information available to us is exploding, along with new tools for communicating, making connections, and sharing knowledge. But with this continual increase in information comes the challenge of how to critically analyze the content, determine what is needed to solve current problems, and transform information into innovative ideas. As we learn more and reassess our knowledge base, information that was once accepted as fact becomes obsolete and is replaced by new findings. These changes can happen very quickly or progress slowly over a long stretch of time. An example of how new scientific information, coupled with advanced satellite telescopes, has led to a change in information is the reclassification of Pluto. Since its discovery in 1930, Pluto was described as the ninth and smallest planet in our solar system. Based on newer findings, in 2006 astronomers redefined the term *planet* and determined that Pluto did not meet all of the characteristics for that designation; Pluto was reclassified as a dwarf planet to "reflect its downgraded status" (Johnson 2006). To make things even more intriguing, in January 2016 evidence of a new planet was announced by two planetary scientists, Konstantin Batygin and Michael Brown (2016). It appears to circle the sun in an elongated orbit, and evidence of its existence is strong. Now, an area of scientific study focused on finding Planet Nine and determining its place in the solar system has emerged. The existence of Planet Nine and other complex questions will be answered as more advanced technology is developed, scientists come up with new theories or refine them to explain their observations, and new information is discovered.

Schools and workplaces need problem solvers who can find solutions to both new problems and existing ones, and who can handle and parse diverse and changing information.

Pink explains that as societies move from the information age—which requires knowledge, expertise, and technical skills—to the *conceptual age*—"an economy and a society built on inventive, empathic, big-picture capabilities"—they need creators and meaning makers who approach problems in unconventional ways (2006, 2). He further describes the need for artistic beauty, interesting narratives, and the ability to combine unrelated ideas into new creations. The new conceptual age, then, requires not only the ability to think of ideas and solutions that no one else is thinking of yet but also the capacity for *high touch*: to empathize, understand human relationships, find joy in self and in others, and search for meaning (Naisbitt 1982; Pink 2006).

Creativity, Innovation, and Meaning Makers

Leaders of business and industry across the world agree that the key to future economic growth is innovation. An IBM survey of more than 1,500 CEOs found that the leadership competency most valued and needed by their organizations is creativity (Bloomberg Business 2010). These CEOs recognize that leaders must think creatively, be adaptable to the changing world, and be willing to experiment with new ideas. In another poll of 5,000 leaders on three continents, 80 percent of respondents reported that unlocking creative potential is the key to economic growth (Adobe Systems 2012).

Florida (2012) notes that as creativity goes, so goes innovation and economic growth. Openness to new ideas and capitalization on people's creative energies have served as the linchpin for many of the United States' past advances and breakthroughs. To continue to prosper, we must invest in developing a creative sector of workers who can think innovatively, are intrinsically motivated, and are able to make independent decisions. Children are the future's scientists, engineers, architects, designers, educators, artists, musicians, business leaders, financiers, and healthcare professionals, and in all of these fields, there is a need for people who can generate new ideas, new technologies, and new content.

In other parts of the world and in some US educational programs, there is a move to make creative development a national priority (Bronson & Merryman 2010). In many countries, creativity is viewed as an important educational learning outcome and has become a major focus. For example, in China, there is an effort to foster the creative spirit and expand the ability to put innovative ideas into practice (Vong 2008). In Australia, creativity is valued as a complex cognitive skill that should be developed (Hui, He, & Liu 2013). In England, there is increased interest in providing a curriculum that specifically includes creative development. A British government report (Craft 2002) states that quality experiences in the early years are the most important aspect in determining a child's success in life and that creativity should be the heart of a program as it is a cornerstone of successful lifelong learning. In both England and Wales, creative/artistic development is one of the seven areas of learning that form the basis for the foundation stage curriculum for children from birth to 5 years old in England and for children from 3 to 7 years old in Wales (GOV.UK 2016; Welsh Government 2015).

The Decline of Creativity in the United States

Americans are often seen as innovators and creative thinkers. However, in 2011 when more than 270,000 adults and children were evaluated with the Torrance Tests of Creative

Thinking (TTCT), their overall creativity scores were significantly lower than those of adults and children who took the TTCT in 1990 (Kim 2011). Kim (2011) concluded that the greatest decline was in children in grades K–3 in the areas of producing ideas (fluency), providing more details (elaboration), and being able to create unique and unusual ideas (originality).

Cecilia's Story

Cecilia just turned 3 years old and attends an early childhood program. Her parents, both successful lawyers, are highly concerned about their daughter's academic preparation because they believe that success in one's career and life is a result of effort and dedication to academics. Cecilia holds her mother's hand firmly as she walks quickly to keep up with her mother's pace. There are only five minutes until her private math class starts at a structured learning academy—an after-school activity her parents decided to enroll Cecilia in twice a week. Cecilia suddenly notices the floor tiles as she walks. The tiles are black and white, and the circular pattern reminds her of a big water swirl. She frees her hand from her mother and jumps in a zigzag motion to avoid the swirl. She giggles in excitement as she jumps and her mother says, "Cecilia, we have no time to play!" Cecilia gives up her pretend play and silently clings to her mother's hand as they enter the math academy.

Story Reflection

In this scenario, Cecilia's mother, intent on her daughter's opportunity to learn in a structured setting, overlooks the potential for learning in Cecilia's playful notice of a pattern in the environment. Teachers and families often feel the pressure of academic demands imposed on children and how it can limit their time for play.

Educators and researchers have tried to determine why there is such a significant decline in the creativity of children in the United States. Some place the blame on external or societal factors. Some suggest that the time many children spend with screens—television, video games, tablets—and in structured activities is crowding out time spent imagining and creating with materials that offer more than one way to play and explore (Hirsh-Pasek et al. 2009; Strasburger, Wilson, & Jordan 2014). Others suggest that it is influenced by the lack of appreciation and value of creativity in early childhood programs and schools (Sawyer 2012). The current emphasis on skills that can be tested and compared rather than on strategies for identifying problems, finding solutions, and investigating topics in depth may be a factor. Many believe that cost-cutting measures responsible for removing the arts—including music, art, drama, and movement programs, as well as attendance of live performances—from schools have negatively impacted creativity (Metla 2015).

Torrance (1962) identifies two powerful inhibitors to children's cognitive development and creative thinking: 1) the premature attempt to eliminate fantasy or play and 2) educational practices that emphasize learning only what is taught. Today, these restraints are still commonly placed on young children and may negatively affect their cognitive development and creative thinking.

Longitudinal research of kindergarten programs from 1998 to 2006 has identified substantial changes in the focus of learning in the classroom (Bassok, Latham, & Rorem 2016). Using national data, the findings show that there is a heightened focus on academic skills, especially reading. During the eight-year study, the amount of time focused on literacy increased by 25 percent; correspondingly, the time spent learning social studies, science, music, art, and physical education dropped significantly. These changes were partially explained by the researchers as increased accountability pressures on the teachers. Even when preschool and kindergarten children were not tested, their teachers experienced intense pressure to prepare students for the assessment they would face in third grade (Bassok, Latham, & Rorem 2016). This decrease in exposure to social studies, science, and the arts comes at a time when young children actually need *more* opportunities to develop their creative thinking, their understanding and appreciation of diversity, their ability to work both independently and collaboratively, and their personal interests and strengths so they can learn the skills needed to cope with and thrive in a rapidly changing world.

A shortage of creative talent is a longstanding problem shared by the United States and other parts of the world is. In this creative age, there must be a worldwide focus on developing and sustaining creative thinking, and supporting people who have powerful ideas. To have a workforce of creative thinkers, we must nurture, renew, and maintain creativity in our education systems, businesses, communities, and societies (Florida 2004).

What Do Today's Children Need for Their Future?

Experts, business leaders, and educators identify several skills and abilities that today's young children need now and in the future (Trilling & Fadel 2009, 8–11; AMA 2010, 3). Children need to be

> **Creative thinkers** who can deal with practical and abstract issues, some of which have not yet even arisen

> **Flexible** and able to adjust to an increasingly complex world filled with information, technology, and diverse people

> **Problem solvers** who will be ready for the challenges and opportunities they will face

> Able to generate **innovative ideas**

With new technology and an ever-expanding, information-based economy, nurturing children's creativity and curiosity while providing a solid foundation in critical thinking, communication, and math is the best way to prepare them for their future (Diamandis & Kotler 2012).

To nurture these skills and abilities, early childhood classrooms must include creative experiences that intrigue children, encourage problem solving, evoke a sense of curiosity and initiative, foster innovative ideas, and include open-ended materials that challenge children's thinking. Young children need opportunities to follow their interests, make choices, collaborate with others, and find meaning in their experiences. They also need teachers who recognize their creative ways of seeing the world and value their growing potential. Children need provocations—invitations to explore an idea or a concept—that match their interests, questions, and actions, and that allow them to gain a deeper understanding of the concepts they are investigating.

The challenge for early childhood educators is establishing an environment where children can, through both teacher- and child-guided experiences, explore, establish goals and plans, work on projects of their own choosing, take responsibility for some of their own learning, search for ideas, question possibilities, probe deeply, try diverse solutions, communicate, revisit and revise their goals, evaluate, and discover excitement in the inventive process. Rather than prepare children to simply follow directions and do well on tests that focus on limited knowledge and skills, we must nurture creative, critical thinkers who are free to make mistakes and encouraged to learn from them. Children need an environment where they are able to expand their thinking and find new possibilities while gaining creative confidence in their abilities. Throughout this process, children also need opportunities to strengthen their social and emotional development with a knowledgeable teacher who values creative thought, supports unique efforts, and plans experiences based on the knowledge and skills she knows children need to develop. Along with experiences in literacy, math, science, and social studies, young children need to pursue the visual arts, music, movement, and drama (Edwards 2010; Fox & Schirrmacher 2015; Isenberg & Durham 2015). Children also need the six aptitudes, or senses, of high touch—design, story, symphony, empathy, play, and meaning (Pink 2006). Teachers weave these elements together in ways that support *every* area of children's learning—intellectual, social and emotional, physical, and creative.

Creativity and Cognition

Creativity can be expressed in diverse ways, from doing a science experiment to writing stories to designing a collage. It can also involve different domains, including cognitive, social, physical, and emotional development, which are reciprocal and interconnected. Many theories of cognitive development include a discussion of creativity, how it impacts intellectual development, and its influence on self-confidence (Csikszentmihalyi 2014; Gardner 2011; Vygotsky 1930).

Theories and approaches to creativity are varied and will be explored in depth in Chapter 2. Several concepts are especially helpful for early childhood educators. As early as 1926, social psychologist and educational theorist Graham Wallas postulated that the creative process was composed of four steps (Runco 2014):

1. Preparation

2. Incubation

3. Illumination

4. Verification

Runco (2014) later added *recursion*, which refers to revisiting the early stages during the creative process and making adjustments as needed, as a fifth step. Understanding these steps helps teachers recognize that the creative process moves through several different levels and that each step has unique features. For example, it is important to recognize that some preparation and planning are needed for creative thinking to occur. Hearing a story told and then discussed can give a child the groundwork she needs to create her own original version of a story. Several days after Luwanda's (age 5) teacher tells a story (incubation), she asks her teacher, "Can I tell you a story?" When Luwanda retells the story, she uses a similar structure, sequence, and the same repetitive phrases as the ones her teacher used, but her story has different characters and takes place in another setting. Luwanda continues to tell her story several times over the next month, and each version varies slightly.

Runco's explanation of recursion also occurs in other areas, such as music. For example, when a musician replays his original song many times to alter (improvise), repeat, or extend it, the improvised song becomes richer, unique, and colorful—just like Luwanda's story.

In other areas, such as science and math, children may not verbalize their thought process. Stephen (age 3) observes his classmates doing a new puzzle his teacher just introduced to the class. He stands near his classmates, but he does not try to do a puzzle on his own or collaborate with his friends. He silently observes the others as they attempt to match the pieces through trial and error for more than half an hour. Three days later, Stephen picks up a challenging new puzzle with many pieces, brings it to the table, and assembles the pieces in less than 10 minutes.

Being creative encourages children to be independent thinkers. During the early years, children need experiences that encourage them to be courageous learners who take risks, try new things, and undertake alternative ways of accomplishing tasks in order to build their confidence (Bruce 2011).

Educating for the Twenty-First Century

In a world that is filled with clocks, schedules, and deadlines, it is essential to understand that creativity happens at its own pace. It cannot be rushed or forced. When a child creates a floating mobile, she needs time to prepare, think, and let the ideas incubate. Once she is into the flow of creating, stopping the effort can have a negative effect on the process. Instead of being tied to a schedule, children need a supportive environment that inspires creative thinking and an adult to observe the children at work, listen to their explanations, offer suggestions and challenges to prompt ideas they have not considered, and provide time for exploration.

The 4Cs

The Partnership for 21st Century Learning (or P21, formerly the Partnership for 21st Century Skills) (NEA 2011), composed of US leaders in education, business, and policy, have identified four skills that they believe are the most important to develop in pre-K–12 education today and that will have a powerful impact on the future of today's children:

> Creativity

> Communication

> Collaboration

> Critical thinking (problem solving)

Together these skills are known as the 4Cs. P21 recommends that educators integrate the 4Cs into classrooms as a way of preparing young people for the demands of their changing world.

Many state and government leaders and numerous professional organizations have supported the inclusion of the 4Cs skills in their educational goals. A National Education Association

(2011) report describes how districts, educators, and teachers can be more purposeful about embedding these competencies in their classrooms and community. A related survey by the American Management Association (2010) found that 80 percent of the participating executives agreed that students would be better prepared to enter the workforce if the 4Cs were integrated into their education. An increased focus on these areas will help today's children be ready for the world in which they will live, work, and participate.

The 4Cs in the Arts

The 4Cs are equally important during the early years and are interrelated, with each positively affecting the other. The arts and other creative experiences provide young children with many opportunities to exercise the 4Cs: developing their creative thinking, communicating about their activities, collaborating with others, and thinking critically.

Offering children open-ended art materials gives them the opportunity to figure out creative ways to use the materials and work with elements such as color, line, shape, and space. As children listen to many different types of music, they learn to discriminate sounds, pitches, rhythms, and patterns and use these elements as they make up their own songs and rhythms. During movement and dance, children problem-solve as they explore physical responses and express their feelings and ideas. Drama and theater activities build children's confidence and communication skills as they share ideas, use more sophisticated oral language, and work with others.

During their experiences with the arts, young children develop relationships, cooperate, and listen to different points of views. In addition, they gain confidence in their social skills and in their ability to regulate their emotions. The arts provide many ways for children to expand their view and knowledge of the world, find new interests, and use their developing skills. Working individually, with a small group of other children, or with adults provides models of creative thinking that can both support and extend children's creative thinking.

Early childhood educators have an amazing opportunity to nurture young children's creative abilities, inspire their thinking, and design an environment that supports their growing capabilities and helps them adapt and succeed in the world. With the guidance of a creative teacher, young children's ideas will be valued, their collaboration encouraged, and their future hopeful.

Reflections

> Has your classroom focus changed in the last few years? How? What do you think about these changes and their impact on young children?

> In what ways are you preparing young children for their future?

> How are you being influenced by accountability in your early childhood environment?

> What new technology is impacting your life and your children's lives? Consider both positive and negative influences.

Michelle (age 4) holds a violin for the first time. Her face lights up when a sound comes from the instrument.

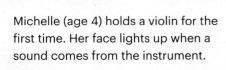

"Gluing Box of Treasures"

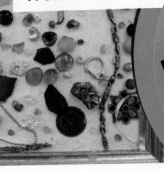

Children's treasures come in various shapes and sizes. Here, they are glued inside a frame and displayed as an artistic creation.

Satomi (age 4) holds her "gluing box of treasures" that boasts a painted gray background, tiny precious stones, and shells of various colors.

"Look what I can do. I can watch the world upside down!" Shari (age 4) shouts with a confident voice. "And I can do it without hands!" Ann (age 5) giggles, adding, "Just like a bat!"

Discovering and Creating Colors

After several days of painting, Rosa (age 4) and Heidi (age 4) return to their creations, discuss how to fill in the white space, and begin experimenting with new shades of colors. They are painting on a canvas with sponges glued to the surface.

They are in awe when they discover that blending blue and red paint makes a beautiful shade of purple.

Rosa and Heidi have created a unique composition that has color, texture, and dimension.

Rosa begins to mix colors and discovers different shades as she paints.

Collage of Collected Materials to Represent Individual Ideas

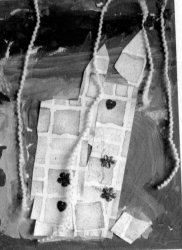

"Rapunzel's Castle" by Madison (age 4)

"The hair is very long. Her dress is purple. She's standing outside in the sun because she let down her hair down the tower. She climbed down her hair."

"The Storm of Death" by John (age 4)

"A big dragon has water and lightning that shoots out from its mouth and fire shoots out from its eyes. He's trying to get a skrill (it's a dragon). It has sharp teeth and three horns. Sharper than a screaming death and bigger, too. It's called sea dragon. It's gigantous maximus. And when its tail splashes in the water, the waves splash twenty feet tall!"

"My House" by Hikari (age 4)

"It's snowing. There's snow in the clouds. It's covering the grass. My family lives there."

"Card Morneit (A Castle Falling Down)" by Zanda (age 4)

"It got knocked by an earthquake. The flowers are really pretty because they didn't get knocked by it. The sky is green because it helps the plants grow."

A display of the children's collages on the wall.

Chapter 2

Understanding the Creative Process

The most important asset you have for negotiating this rapidly changing world is your creative brain.

—Shelley Carson, *Your Creative Brain: Seven Steps to Maximize Imagination, Productivity, and Innovation in Your Life*

The first step to understanding creativity is to learn about the creative process. Theorists, researchers, writers, and scholars who have studied and discussed the creative process offer many ways to identify, observe, and support the development of creativity. According to Jervis and Tobier (1988), the principal goal of education is to foster the development of men and women who are capable of making and doing new things—who create, invent, and make discoveries, not simply repeat what past generations have done. Teaching, therefore, as Patty Smith Hill noted, should involve creative thinking (Fowlkes 1992; Lascarides & Hinitz 2000).

Dewey identified four tendencies that precipitate learning (Dewey 1915; Wolfe 2000):

> Social (communicating with others)

> Constructive (making things)

> Investigative and experimental (finding out about things)

> Expressive (creating things)

These are often woven into creative activities and support generating ideas, making models, trying different possibilities, and describing products.

"Creativity becomes more visible when adults try to be more attentive to the cognitive processes of children than to the results they achieve in various fields of doing and understanding" (Edwards, Gandini, & Forman 1998, 77). However, because creativity involves complex ways of thinking and often results in doing things in unique ways, the process is more difficult to study or measure than its products or achievements. Thus, many writers and researchers have investigated four identifiable dimensions of creativity:

> The creative person

> The creative process

> The environment

> The product of creativity

While many studies focus on creative adults and their work, information from these studies provide insights into the creative process that young children also use, some of which are discussed in this chapter.

Creativity is often considered a trait possessed by only a few highly talented individuals whose ideas have dramatically changed the world in some way. Among those frequently mentioned are scientists like Albert Einstein, who developed the theory of relativity, and artists who developed new techniques, such as Pablo Picasso and his use of cubes or Martha Graham and her form of modern dance. This exceptional level of creativity, which sets the bar very high—so high that few people can attain it—is referred to as *Big-C* (Kaufman & Beghetto 2009). Big-C identifies work that has revolutionized an aspect of life for many people, or has developed or changed a way of thinking. Kaufman and Beghetto also identified another type of creativity that is within the grasp of a much broader range of people—*little-c*. Little-c is personal creativity used in everyday life, and it is important, recognizable, and can have positive benefits for individuals and the environment. For example, young children can build a unique outdoor structure by combining stones, wood, and pieces of canvas. Since this is the

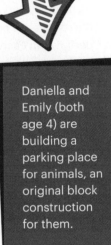

first time they have built a structure in this way, it can be identified as creative for these children. They are using a construction process that can be observed, identified, and valued. An early childhood teacher may develop a class website so that the children's work can be shared with their families. The design of this website reflects the teacher's creativity as she navigates a new way to communicate with families. During the process, she outlines possible strategies and makes many decisions that challenge her to think in new ways while using different software tools. Throughout the design phase, and later when incorporating additional information, her creative thinking will be challenged again and again.

You may think, "Oh, I'm not creative," but you are. You develop ideas, have interactions, and plan learning opportunities throughout the day that expand your own thinking and the thinking of the children you educate. Personal creativity is trying something that you have never done before, doing familiar tasks in new ways, or elaborating on an idea. For instance, you might make handmade paper out of recycled materials and extend the idea by adding flower petals, leaves, and colorful threads. Recognizing this type of creativity, an example of little-c, helps you see children's inventiveness as well as value your own creativity.

Process Is King

Ryan, who is 5 years old, wants to create accessories to use in dramatic play. He explores the junk box to find materials he can use to make his king's crown, cloak, and jewels. When he has finished making them, he goes to the dramatic play center to carry out his mission as the "king of the world." When he is finished playing, he dismantles his creations and puts them back in the junk box piece by piece. In the art learning center, Melody, who is 4 years old, builds a remarkable sand structure on a tray. The structure has intricate details, like windows, a staircase, and a moat. After she finishes her work, she pours a bottle of water over her creation, just to see what happens. The various parts of the complex structure meld into each other and become a wet pile of sand.

In both of these creative projects there is no enduring product to be admired, but creativity was an essential part of each process. The idea that the process is more important than the product shapes your perception of creativity as you observe, support, and respond to young children. What does this principle mean, and why is it essential for teachers to understand it?

As you work with young children, it is critical to recognize that not every creative effort will result in a product to display or exhibit. Some activities, projects, and experiments do not have a final product—perhaps because the child, like Ryan, dismantles his efforts, or because in the process of experimentation the "product" evolves and changes and does not last, as in Melody's case. What children think and what they do as they engage in an activity—and how their thinking develops and matures as a result—are the most important aspects of the experience. Some creative activities, however, do result in a product. The distinction is that children select the materials, tools, and techniques to produce their own unique results. The final product is not predetermined by the teacher or copied from another's work, but is instead one of a kind—such as a collage of twigs and clay a child collected during outdoor play. If the main focus of the teacher is the final product, then the steps, experimentation, and trials during the process may be seen as a distraction from the desired goal of making a beautiful display or arriving

Daniella and Emily (both age 4) are building a parking place for animals, an original block construction for them.

at a predetermined outcome. If, instead, you value children's creativity and the process of exploration, you support these experiences and encourage children's individual efforts.

By observing the process children use, listening to their language, and documenting their work, you can recognize that they are creating and thinking in complex ways during the entire experience. When your focus is on the children, their creative thinking process, the steps they implement, and the ways you can support their creativity, children are more likely to feel encouraged to keep experimenting instead of being concerned about whether or not they have "correctly" accomplished something you wanted them to reproduce.

Hiro's Story

Three-year-old Hiro is painting at an easel with tempera paint using a small paint roller. Experimenting with yellow and blue, he finds that lines and patterns can be made by varying the way he moves the roller across the canvas. He continues painting and reinventing the design with each additional roll. Hiro is mesmerized by the ways the color and shape change as the roller responds to his movements. Finally, his canvas is covered with paint and the entire picture is blue. Displaying no dismay that he now has a big blue picture, Hiro looks at his picture and smiles.

Hiro (age 3) explores colors, lines, and patterns using a paint roller.

Later, Hiro returns to the art area and searches for the small paint roller. This time he selects different paint colors—red and black—and proceeds to experiment with creating thin, thick, and zigzagging lines.

Hiro's teacher comes up beside him and remarks, "I see you have many different kinds of lines on your painting." After another minute, when Hiro pauses in his painting, the teacher points to a specific spot and asks, "I wonder how you made this curve happen."

Story Reflection

Hiro carefully chooses the colors and tools he wants to create his painting. As he observes how the paint responds to the way he moves the roller, he experiments with different ways to move it and add color to the paper. He watches the patterns he produces with the roller.

All of this investigation and flexible thinking helps Hiro discover attributes of color, line, pattern, and design. This experience boosts his creative confidence because he is able to act upon his ideas and the materials at hand.

Hiro's teacher supports his efforts by asking thoughtful questions about his experimentation and using language to describe his methods of producing patterns. Although Hiro doesn't need another person's evaluation of his painting, his teacher's comments help him think about his work and learn language related to the process.

Wallas's Early Model of Creative Thinking

Graham Wallas's (1926) ideas on creative thinking have been expanded on and discussed by many other writers, including Carson (2010), Guilford (1967), and Ward and Saunders

(2003). The Wallas model shows that gaining information and resources is a vital first step in the creative process. Rarely do brilliant ideas just pop into our minds, and Wallas and Carson help us understand the process of nurturing creative thinking.

The steps in the creative process that were introduced in Chapter 1—preparation, incubation, illumination, and verification—are similar to those used by researchers in diverse fields. You can also use them to guide the creative process in your setting.

Preparation

Children's creative quests often begin with a problem or question, identified by either themselves or by the teacher. To explore or investigate that problem or question, the children might start by discussing what they already know, suggesting some ideas, and then gathering information through field trips, books, or interviews with people who have knowledge about the topic. This phase should engage children's interest, expand their knowledge, and begin to define and refine the problem or question. For example, a group of young children are concerned that the plants in their terrarium are turning brown. Noticing the children's concern, their teacher asks, "What can we do to help the plants grow?" To answer the question, the children and the teacher research how to solve it by looking up information in books and on websites about plants and soil, and by interviewing some knowledgeable individuals.

Incubation

To help children digest all the information they've gathered and develop it into actions they might take, a teacher might suggest taking a break from actively researching and encourage children to think about the issue and what they've learned so far. When children think about ideas or incubate possibilities, they can look like they aren't focusing, or even like they're daydreaming, but this is an important step in the creative process. Some children may have an idea in mind but need to find the materials or take some time to consider how it might work. Others will want to try out a solution right away. By being an alert observer, you can recognize when a child is developing an idea, looking around at materials to activate a thought, or turning over a possible approach in her mind.

Illumination

This step is often described as the light bulb effect or insight—the "aha!" moment. Children discover a new idea or combination of ideas that address the problem or question. You might hear children say, "Let's do this!" or "This will work!"

Verification

During the final phase of the creative process, children experiment with the solution they identified in the illumination stage to see if it will work. Experimenting consists of three parts: evaluation (determining if the solution works), elaboration (expanding the idea), and implementation (doing something with the idea). This stage might include making a construction, a chart, an action, a drama, or an artistic creation. To help children evaluate their solution, you might take photographs of the process, observe and write down the actions they take, and document their language and ask questions to help further their thinking. During this step, children might realize that they need to take a different approach entirely, or that they just need to refine or adjust their original solution.

Cassandra's Story

Cassandra is aware that many of the children in her preschool classroom live in the community around the school but have limited experience outside their homes. She wants the children to become familiar with their neighborhood and the area around the preschool program. She knows that the community is diverse, has varied businesses, and contains many interesting people who will help the children appreciate their neighborhood. Cassandra decides to use the creative process steps to help the children become better acquainted with their community.

Preparation. The problem Cassandra identifies is that the children do not know their neighborhood well. During large group time, she and the children discuss the neighborhood where they live. The children examine printed materials such as restaurant menus, flyers, local newspapers, and maps about some of the businesses and services in the community. Then, they take a walk through their neighborhood and collect information as they look at the houses, shops, and other interesting features. During their excursion, they talk to people they see and sketch some of the buildings and architecture. Afterward, they discuss some ways to use and share their information, such as a mural, a collection of stories from people interviewed, and maps of the neighborhood.

Incubation. For the next few days, the children take a break from the active investigation of their neighborhood. Some children discuss their walk during this time, but Cassandra does not focus on what they saw or learned.

Illumination. Several days later, during group time, Cassandra and the children talk about their walk through their neighborhood. They review the sketches they made, brochures they collected, and the people they talked to during the trip. They discuss how to share the information they gained, how to represent the streets and buildings that are in their neighborhood, and how to display their findings. Several children make new suggestions: to take more pictures, make a video, interview a storekeeper, invite a neighbor to the class, and visit the children's homes or community buildings. Ultimately, they decide to create a map of the neighborhood that will provide a view of the streets, important buildings, and include the locations of their homes.

Verification. Cassandra provides a large sheet of butcher paper and a variety of materials and tools for the children to use to design their map. The children create drawings or three-dimensional structures to represent their homes, which they later attach to the map. Some children also draw or create an interesting shop, a public building, or street signs. While working, they identify other special features to add as the investigation continues, like parks, churches, hospitals, post offices, fire stations, stoplights, trees, bike trails, and benches. Over the course of the next several weeks, the children continue to add important elements to their map and talk about adding other features. They display the map in their classroom so they can revisit it, continue to add additional features, and let others see the representation of their community.

Story Reflection

After identifying the problem, Cassandra's goal is for the children to learn about the neighborhood in which they live. During the project they gain information about their neighborhood, look at local maps, and explore resources in the area. They examine books and pictures that feature neighborhoods similar to theirs. The children and teacher collaborate to determine the best way to represent their neighborhood and decide on a map. Together they find ways to represent their homes and other buildings in their neighborhood. The children change and adapt their ideas many times as they work individually, with partners, and in small groups. Ultimately they develop a map that reflects what they learned about their community—the roads, the buildings, the special features, the services, and the people who live and work there. When evaluating the project, they decide to add to what the class had originally created.

During this creative experience, the children use spatial reasoning (math) and problem-solving skills (science, math, and construction), and they expand their language by learning new vocabulary and communicating with their classmates and members of the community (language and literacy). They also extend their understanding of the composition and diversity of the community where they live (social studies). They gain an appreciation of their community and the unique people who live close to them.

Ruth (age 4) is adding details to the building that she is going to include in the map.

Cassandra shares several maps with the children and discusses the neighborhood and the community.

Allison and Ruth (both age 4) are collaborating to connect a path between their neighborhood buildings.

Torrance's View of the Creative Process

An early pioneer in the study of creativity in young children, E. Paul Torrance identified four elements of the creative process: originality, flexibility, fluency, and elaboration. These are still used today (Sawyer 2012) and reflect the process of both children and adults. These elements are also used extensively in the Torrance Tests of Creative Thinking, which are frequently used to examine the creative process. Although these elements are not all-inclusive, they do provide specific ways to recognize and identify the creative process in young children and adults.

Originality is creating an idea, procedure, or product that is unique for a particular child or in relation to other children at a similar stage of development. When asked to name some things that are red, a 4-year-old might say an apple, a cardinal in the yard, and his older sister's poison ivy rash!

Fluency is the generation of many ideas with a focus on producing numerous possible options or solutions. For example, a child might use small, empty boxes as houses, wagons, storage, treasure containers, earphones, a bed for a tiny doll, a container for a bug—the possibilities are endless.

Flexibility is the ability to change direction and move from one way of thinking about an issue to another. For example, thinking in different ways and exploring alternatives helps 3-year-old Charlie in his search for a microphone to use on the classroom stage. He begins by using a marker that he holds in his hand; however, he is not satisfied with this microphone, so he tries making something else. He finds a small plastic ball in a bin in the science area. He places the ball on the top of the marker and covers both objects with aluminum foil. Although the foil holds the ball in place on the marker, the combination is shaky and he is not happy with the results. He tries a different approach, this time using masking tape to hold the ball and marker together. Next, he reattaches the foil to cover the entire piece, and his microphone is complete. When a young child, like Charlie, begins with one idea, changes to another, and then modifies it, he is demonstrating flexible thinking.

"Farmer robot" is attractively displayed to highlight the special creation. It demonstrates to the child that her work is valued.

Meg (age 4) says, "It turns into a robot . . . transforms into a farmer. Once it is a farmer, it plants corn. The water turns into milk. Ice cream comes through the purple thing."

Elaboration is taking an idea and expanding it to make it more complex or interesting. Teachers often do this when they get ideas from a book, website, or another teacher. Julia, a preschool teacher, might think "Oh, this isn't my idea," but when another teacher notices the interesting way Julia has displayed the children's pictures, she admits, "Well, I did change it a bit. I used broken bits of shells around the frames instead of foil," or "I didn't have much wall space, so I hung them on coat hangers." She was inspired by an idea she saw for how to display children's work and adapted it to work in her environment. This elaboration of an existing idea demonstrates her creative thinking.

Divergent and Convergent Thinking

The creative process includes both divergent and convergent thinking. *Divergent thinking*—following many lines of thought and expanding ideas—is used to come up with many ways to do something or many possible answers to a problem. *Convergent thinking* involves narrowing many possibilities to choose the best solution for a situation. There may be times that children go back and forth between the two types, employing divergent thinking again when a selected solution does not work or needs tweaking. For example, a small group of children are working with their teacher to figure out how to display the new pictures of each child in the classroom. The children offer a number of possibilities, such as sticking the pictures on the windowpanes, hanging them from a pole from the ceiling, collecting them in a book, using rope to string them across the room, and taping them to their cubbies (divergent thinking). Together, they decide to put the pictures in clear plastic bags and hang them from a colored line across the width of the room (convergent thinking). As they carry out their plan, they discover that the line they were planning to use is not long enough to go across the entire room. What to do? Again the children offer suggestions, including buying another clothesline, adding some thick yarn from the art center or colored electrical wire to lengthen the clothesline, or putting the display in a corner of the room (divergent thinking). Ultimately they decide to put the pictures in one corner of the room using different colors of electrical wire (convergent thinking). In the classroom and in life, both convergent and divergent thinking are needed to work out problems and find solutions.

Ask questions that encourage children to think in different ways (divergent thinking). Some examples of divergent questions, for which no right answer is expected or rewarded, are "What else could we use?," "What could we add?," and "What other ways could we display our pictures?" Although divergent thinking is not synonymous with creative thinking, it does help us understand the cognitive processes that can lead to creativity (Runco 2014).

Of course, there are many types of problems and diverse ways to solve them. For example, a teacher has no glue for the art project she was planning (the problem), so she mixes flour with water. The children can use this sticky mixture to attach paper to a group mural (a solution). Sometimes the problem may not be recognized by others or clearly defined. For example, an artist may want to find another medium or technique to express an idea or show a colorful sunset. In these situations, it is recognizable that creativity is not just generating problems but finding solutions to problems.

"The alligator is sharing his lunch with the fish and the caribou. They were very hungry, but now they are all friends."

Bryan's Story

Maria, a Head Start teacher, selects a science activity to introduce the concept of water flow to the 4-year-olds she teaches. She places several materials in the water table, including small pots and pans, strainers, plastic containers, and bottles with various shapes and opening sizes. She also adds blue food coloring to the water so children can see its movement better. Soon, children surround the enticing table and begin to explore by scooping, pouring, squeezing, splashing, and dumping the water. Some children stack the available materials upside down to make a tower, pour water from the top of the tower, and giggle as they see the stream of water flowing down. Others repeat the motion of dumping and pouring into several different containers and bottles. Bryan—one of the explorers—becomes frustrated because the water he is pouring is not going inside a bottle. He does not notice that the bottle opening is small, so when he tries to pour water into it, the water goes everywhere except inside the bottle. Maria observes Bryan and quietly adds a plastic funnel to the water table near him. Bryan experiments with the funnel and shows surprise when the water comes out as a thin stream from the bottom stem. Eventually, he connects the new object with his problem and successfully uses the funnel as a tool to pour water inside the bottle with the small opening. After the exploration period, Maria poses some questions for extending the children's examination of the water and tools: "What other containers could we add to our water table?," "How would you transfer the water from this container to that bottle?," and "How can you make the stream of water narrower or wider?"

Story Reflection

Maria's goal is for children to engage in a scientific exploration of water flow by using intentionally selected materials to explore and solve any problems that arise. Maria adds a funnel to scaffold Bryan's efforts when he experiences a problem in his explorations. Instead of directly telling Bryan the answer to his problem, Maria casually places the funnel near him so that he can explore, examine, and find his own solution to the problem. This kind of open-ended activity and teacher responsiveness help children develop their creative thinking and gain confidence in their problem-solving skills. Maria also extends the children's thinking by asking questions. Later, she reflects with the children about how the new objects, materials, and color influence the water flow.

Right Brain, Left Brain, or Both?

Many theorists and researchers, including Feldman (1980), Amabile (1983), and Isaksen (1987), have focused their attention on cognition as they studied the internal mental process and intrinsic motivations that occur while people are engaged in the creative process. From 1970 to 1990, researchers had few ways to observe the inner workings of the brain, so many experimental procedures were used to help infer its functions and activity levels during the creative process.

Bryan (age 4) knows how to pour water into the large container without spilling, but not into the bottle with a smaller opening. The teacher introduces the yellow funnel to the water table to encourage further exploration.

Currently, brain imaging tools, including magnetic resonance imaging (MRI), positron emission tomography (PET), and single-photon emission computed tomography (SPECT), provide new insights into the creative process, fueling upsurges of interest in how the brain develops and works during creative activity. Classic studies, such as Gazzaniga and Sperry's (1967) work with patients whose brain hemispheres functioned independently of each other, as well as recent work in neuroscience (see Vartanian, Bristol, & Kaufman 2013), help us better understand the connection between brain functioning and creative thinking.

The right and left hemispheres of the brain are connected by a remarkable network of neurons called the corpus callosum, which allows the hemispheres to communicate with each other. Although it was once believed that the right hemisphere was the center of creativity, the current thinking is that both sides of the brain are necessary for creativity. As Harvard professor and researcher Shelley Carson (2010) notes, creative thinking is so complex that it involves multiple acts that use many circuits throughout the brain. While she cautions that no area or hemisphere of the brain works alone—each is dependent on connections made to other areas—Carson does believe that there are some areas in the brain particularly important to creativity. Among the many different regions, she suggests there is an executive control center, which is the area "in charge of planning, abstract reasoning, and conscious decision-making" (Carson 2010, 46). These skills are necessary for the development of scientific study, innovative projects, and communication in many different forms. In the planning step of the creative process, for example, individuals collect information, determine what questions will be posed, and decide approaches to be implemented. During the entire investigation, they make numerous decisions, adaptations and changes, and conclusions.

Creativity scholar Mark Runco (2014) too explains, "There is no one 'seat' of creativity in the brain, or responsible location or even hemisphere. Creativity . . . draws on many different brain structures and processes" (71–72). Mihov, Denzler, and Förster (2010) suggest that the right hemisphere is better at exploring new possibilities, while the left hemisphere is better at applying previously learned concepts. In their review of a number of studies, Mihov and colleagues conclude that holistic (global) thinking, context-dependent thinking, and thinking using figures or drawings is dominated by the right hemisphere. In addition, they suggest that subprocesses, such as the development of a problem, gathering information, and incubation, predominately happen in the right hemisphere.

Based on current research, it can be concluded that creativity requires both hemispheres of the brain and uses specific areas of the brain during complex and integrated processes. When children learn something new or participate in a creative activity, the neurons in their brain form new connections. In fact, learning and creating actually change the brain and help build a richer, denser network of connections (Carson 2010).

Creativity is not a result of cognitive processes alone; it is also influenced by the "emotional brain"—motivation, attitude, interest, feelings of security, and persistence. Although the emotional brain plays an essential role in creativity, the creative process also requires systems and interactions among other structures and areas of the brain (Runco 2014).

Creativity and Stages of Development

Theorists have described the development of children as occurring in stages (e.g., Erickson 1980; Piaget & Inhelder 1969). There is a spectrum of individual differences in the progression through these stages, influenced by children's environment, experiences, capabilities, relationships with other people, and range of opportunities (Kohlberg 1984).

Lawrence Kohlberg's (1984) work on moral reasoning has been used to understand different domains related to creativity, such as art and language, in addition to divergent thinking. Kohlberg notes that young children are in the preconventional stage. During this stage, young children are uninhibited by rules or the expectations of others. They play, use language, explore concepts, and try artistic techniques by following their individual interests and ideas. This means that their artwork, projects, and experiments are self-expressive, may be unconventional, and are often very creative. Children are able to act on their own ideas and produce unique results because they have little concern for how others evaluate their efforts. By age 9 or 10, children become more sensitive to conventions and grow more interested in conforming to rules and social expectations. Runco points to this as a possible explanation for why younger children are often very creative while many older children seem to experience a slump in their creativity (Runco 2014).

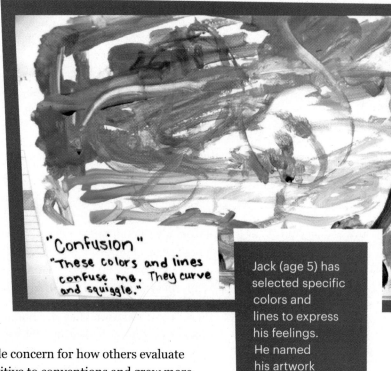

"Confusion"

"These colors and lines confuse me. They curve and squiggle."

Jack (age 5) has selected specific colors and lines to express his feelings. He named his artwork "Confusion."

Recent Examination of Creative Thinking

Project Zero, a five-year project at the Harvard Graduate School of Education, explored ways to nurture thinking in school settings. To make thinking more visible, scholars Ritchhart, Church, and Morrison (2011, 11) identified six kinds of thinking that are involved in fostering the understanding of new ideas:

1. Observing closely and describing what is there

2. Building explorations and interpretations

3. Reasoning with evidence

4. Making connections

5. Considering different viewpoints and perspectives

6. Capturing the heart (core) of the idea and forming conclusions

Although some of the ideas presented in their writings are more appropriate for older children, several can be used to develop a culture of thinking that is also appropriate for early childhood settings. For example, you might use the first kind of thinking—observing closely and describing what is there—to enrich opportunities for children to pay attention to and use language to express what they see. A group of children found a small bird nest being constructed in the opening of the playground fence. Over the next several weeks, the children observed the mother bird building and adding intriguing materials, such as twine, scraps of colorful fabric and paper, wire, and straw. When they were on the playground, they asked a lot of questions: "How big is the nest going to be?," "Will there be eggs in the nest?," "How many?," and "When will we see the baby birds?" Careful observation over time helped these children identify and describe the transformation of the nest by using their language, writing in journals, and drawing what they saw. You can use some of these strategies to nurture young children's thinking and help their creativity become more visible.

Other ways to expand children's understanding and get them thinking about further possibilities are questioning, listening, and documenting.

Questioning

Teachers know the importance of asking good, thought-provoking questions. Bloom's taxonomy (Bloom 1984), which has been revised by Anderson and Krathwohl (2001), is a progression of lower- to higher-level thinking skills—remembering, understanding, applying, analyzing, evaluating, and creating. Asking effective questions moves thinkers to higher-level skills that require more complex thinking, such as analyzing, evaluating, and creating.

Fusco (2012) suggests that questioning should be flexible to allow teachers to both show their interest in children's ideas and to scaffold children in constructing their own understanding. You can help children clarify their thinking by focusing your questions on what they are doing or saying, demonstrating that you are attentive to their thinking. This type of questioning and support moves beyond the memory level and avoids making children find the answer you have in mind. *Productive questions* include inquiries for which you don't know the answer or have a predetermined answer. Such questions "take a student forward in his or her thinking; they enable a teacher to provide scaffolding for students beginning to build their own understandings" (Martens 1999, 25). As you engage young children in discussing their thinking processes, you will shape, change, and refocus your questions. Table 2.1 shows several examples of productive questions (Elstgeest 2001; Martens 1999).

Table 2.1. Six Types of Productive Questions

Types	Examples
Attention-focusing question	What have you noticed about . . .? Have you seen . . .? Where do you notice . . .?
Measuring and counting question	How far did . . .? How high/low do you . . .? How many did . . .?
Comparison question	How do these . . .? Which one . . .? Is there a difference when you . . .? How are these alike/different?
Action question	What could you do? What happens if you . . .? What's next?
Problem-posing question	How can you make . . .? What can you do to . . .? What else can you do . . .?
Reasoning question	I wonder why . . .? Why do you think . . .?

Although questions are an excellent way to encourage children to explain their thoughts and consider different solutions or ways of thinking, asking children too many questions may inhibit their responses or interrupt their thought processes. Before you ask children questions, it is important to listen to their conversations. Alternating asking questions with listening attentively will help you determine the appropriate time to ask a thoughtful question.

Listening

As you ask children questions, remember to really listen to their responses. As an active listener, demonstrate your interest in the children's ideas and your openness to different possibilities rather than listening for the expected, "right" answer. For example, let a child know you are interested in her ideas by saying, "That is an interesting idea about _____," "I understand what you are saying; tell me more," "You are really thinking about this," or "What are you going to do next?" If you don't understand the child's explanation, make a statement or ask another question to help him explore his reasoning: "Tell me what you are thinking," "Will you explain what you are doing?," "I would like to hear more about this project."

Linda attentively listens to the child's story during the story table activities. She is recording each of the children's actions and words.

Active listening conveys respect for the child's ideas, shows interest in his suggestions, and supports his attempts to try new things. This is far more effective than simple affirmative or neutral comments or nodding your head. Another positive benefit of active listening is that when your responses relate to children's thinking, they are more likely to feel comfortable sharing their ideas. In addition, you are modeling this listening technique for other children in the classroom to use with their peers, engendering an attitude of trust and respect.

Documenting

Documentation, which may include "observing, recording, interpreting, and sharing" the thinking process in order to deepen learning (Given et al. 2010, 38), is another important way to understand children's thinking. To document children's work you might record or write children's words, photograph a process, or collect and assemble their work into a portfolio or display. By using such tools as documentation panels—presentation boards that display evidence and artifacts of children's learning—children and teachers explore, examine, and enrich their thinking. For example, a teacher and a group of young children interested in fish and other forms of sea life visit a local aquarium. How can the children remember and share their favorite experiences with their classmates or guardians? Some children suggest taking pictures or sketching the fish, while others mention video recording and journaling. During the visit, the teacher asks questions, takes notes, records the children's conversations, and takes photographs. They later assemble their artifacts into a documentation panel.

Effective documentation provides a visible way to understand and recognize children's thinking. Chapter 8 includes a more detailed discussion of documentation.

Early childhood educators have the fascinating opportunity to work with children who are very creative, express their ideas in many different ways, and discover unique solutions to problems or questions. Cherish children's surprising ideas and actively listen to their marvelous explanations. Endeavor to understand their thinking as they enthusiastically participate in personally meaningful activities and progress through the creative process. As a teacher and learner, you will gain new insight into the creative process by observing and interacting with young children.

Reflections

> Think about a time you observed a young child painting or using other art media where you saw the creative process at work. What aspects of the creative process did you observe?

> Describe a time when children used open-ended materials and created a product, or perhaps when they used these flexible materials to experiment or explore but there was no final product. What are your thoughts about these two different experiences?

> Have you observed a child who self-evaluates his or her work with little concern about what you or others think?

> How can you help children evaluate their own work, recognizing positive aspects as well as ways to grow or find new direction?

> Think of ways you can support children in making choices related to their work.

> How can you use the steps in the creative problem-solving process with children? How will you help children refine their thinking skills?

Evidence of Creating, Thinking, and Learning

Before Todd (age 4) begins the development of his robot, he makes a plan for how it will look and work.

After making a plan, he searches through the loose parts to find flexible pieces that can be used for the robot's arms.

Next, Todd puts glue on the discarded doorbell so he can attach the arms.

After Todd finishes his robot, his teacher displays his hugging robot and a related documentation panel in the hall of his center.

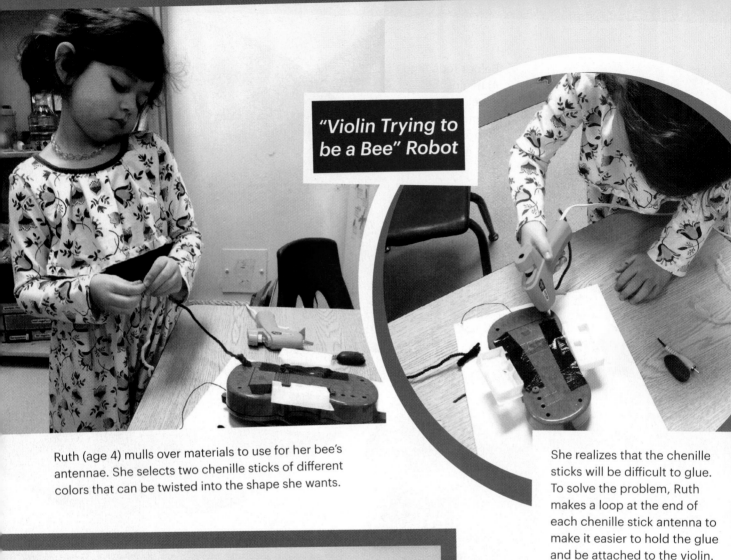

"Violin Trying to be a Bee" Robot

Ruth (age 4) mulls over materials to use for her bee's antennae. She selects two chenille sticks of different colors that can be twisted into the shape she wants.

She realizes that the chenille sticks will be difficult to glue. To solve the problem, Ruth makes a loop at the end of each chenille stick antenna to make it easier to hold the glue and be attached to the violin.

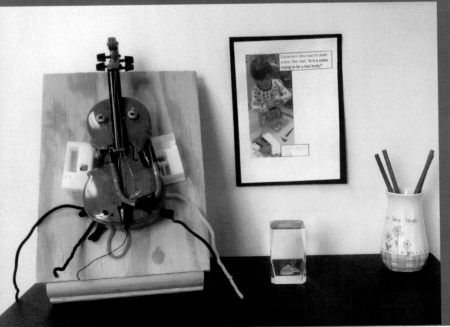

The display of the violin bee includes pictures of Ruth and the words she used to describe her creation: "It is a violin trying to be a bee body!"

Chapter 3

The Environment:
A Look Inside Classrooms
That Inspire Creativity

*Our goal . . . is to create places
of freedom and delight where the
enchantments and mysteries of
childhood can be given full expression.*

—**Anita Olds**, *Child Care Design Guide*

It is Angelica's (age 4) first day of preschool. She stands in the classroom doorway, anxiously scanning the room to see what the space is like and what is happening there. As she slowly ventures into this unfamiliar place, she notices that it's filled with sparkling sunlight, which is reflected off of large mirrors scattered around the room. Brightly colored pictures dance on the walls and hang from the ceiling. Angelica is captivated by the interesting materials she sees. Some are familiar (there is an area filled with items similar to those in her family's kitchen), and others she is curious to know more about (enormous blocks, tiny figures, and a large piece of glittery purple fabric stretched to the top of a tall structure). She hears children singing and laughing at the funny words of a song.

A smiling woman comes over to Angelica and welcomes her to the class. She explains what is happening in the classroom and invites Angelica to go to the library area and look at a book, join the class for community time on the soft rug, or play with the pinecones, leaves, acorns, and shiny pebbles that are displayed on a table. As Angelica ponders these choices, she notices a small round table with an arrangement of sunflowers in a colorful container in the center. Also on the table are apple slices and small pieces of cheese on a shiny tray. Are the apples and cheese for her to eat when she is hungry? Her body relaxes as she begins to see that this classroom is a safe place with nice, caring people who provide interesting experiences that she will enjoy.

The early childhood environment has a tremendous impact on children's learning, behavior, and creative development. The environment communicates many different things to children—what happens there, what is important, and what they will be able to experience. The physical environment also reflects the values of the teacher who sets up the space, chooses the challenging materials and books to display, and thoughtfully plans to incorporate a variety of experiences that match the children's interests and capabilities.

The composition and values of the community, including the children, their families, and teachers, also influence how the space functions, where interactions occur, and how adjustments are made to nurture children's creative efforts. The environment provides opportunities for communicating, building relationships, solving problems, and pursuing creative work. Because each classroom environment reflects a diverse group of children, the larger community, and a particular program philosophy, it will have a unique design with a distinctive look and features.

The early childhood environment has a tremendous impact on children's learning, behavior, and creative development.

The environment affects the creative thinking that takes place there as well. For example, an invention center displays a collection of interesting materials in bins that resemble a workshop and a low table where innovators can work. Some of the items included in this area are child-size tools (e.g., pliers, screwdriver, clamps, scissors, protective work glasses, and gloves) and materials (e.g., wood scraps, cardboard tubes, electrical wire, pipe cleaners, foil, string, macramé rope, and nuts or bolts). Children explore and create in this area based on their own ideas, or they work together with others. A large corkboard in the area contains pictures and illustrations depicting famous inventors and their work, and a small bench displays several fiction and nonfiction books on related subjects. In addition, there are sketches and designs the children make in planning their creations. These collections support children's budding ideas.

An outdoor invention center provides space, tools, and materials for children to plan and work on the projects of their choice.

The following information about early childhood environments focuses on design features, grouping, and materials you can use to support children's creative thinking. Because young children have diverse interests and abilities, your classroom environment needs to have a variety of choices to support and challenge them.

Environments That Support Creative Thinking

Children's positive attitudes about learning are shaped by classroom environments where they feel welcome, safe, cared for, and valued. The environment should be homelike and inviting so that children feel comfortable to be active and engaged in meaningful experiences. A well-organized space makes it clear to children where materials belong and what choices they have.

There are many ways to make the children and adults feel like they are part of the classroom community. For example, many Reggio Emilia–inspired classrooms have an attractive arrangement of photographs of the children, clearly showing that the focus of the program is on them. Another way to make children feel valued is by prominently displaying their creations for their classmates and others to appreciate. In such environments, children frequently say to visitors, "Wanna see my picture?" or "Look what I made!," revealing their pride in the displays about them and their community of learners.

Teachers put their own stamp on the classroom space. For instance, he might put together a collage or display area with his picture and other things that represent what is important to him, such as photos of his family or pet or excerpts from his favorite books. This display inspires questions and comments from children and their families, which helps them connect with the teacher and build the positive relationships that are so important in providing emotional support for young children.

A hanging collection of each child's picture helps the children develop a sense of community and belonging.

Two children look at the teacher's personal display in the hallway.

Creating a Vision

An environment that cultivates creative thinking begins with a plan to develop a beautiful, intriguing place for young children. There are many things to consider:

> How do you want children to see the space?

> What kinds of play and thinking might be inspired there?

> What feelings should be stimulated?

> What options can you provide for children who are exploding with ideas?

> Will there be a gathering place for a small group of learners?

> Will you include a quiet space where children can slow down and incubate an idea?

> How can the environment reflect the children and their families?

> What features make your classroom space unique?

> How can you change the environment as new interests and projects develop?

Your vision and design of the environment affect children's responses, support their ideas, and encourage their engagement in meaningful experiences. Throughout the year, change or adjust different areas of the classroom to keep the environment fresh, exciting, and challenging. The space is also transformed by children as they learn and work in it. Families, teachers, and peers will be able to see what the children are creating, learn what they are working on, and perhaps read displays or listen to recordings of what the children have to say about their work.

Planning an Effective Environment

At the beginning of each year, think about your space and its arrangement. What learning do you want the environment to encourage? If you want the environment to inspire artistic creativity, does the art area include a variety of materials, an attractive way to display work, and a place where a child can store her work so she can continue to work on it later? If you want children to experiment with movement, is there a space where this can happen and props that support movement? Intentionally plan the environment so these opportunities are possible, and then during the year, observe how the children use the spaces. Is it what you envisioned? Are more interesting activities transpiring then you had imagined? If these new, unanticipated uses are meaningful for you and the children, make adjustments, rearrange areas, or add new spaces as needed. The environment is transformed by the way children choose to make use of it, and in turn, you support children's learning and development with careful planning, reflection, and adjustment throughout the year.

A Beautiful Place

Young children and their teachers should work and learn in a classroom environment that nurtures an appreciation for beauty, contains intriguing items, and includes displays that make learning visible. "The quality and aesthetics of materials, furnishings, and images . . . help the child appreciate, love, respect, and take advantage of the environment" (Edwards & Gandini 2015, 97). To create such an environment, provide many opportunities for you and the children to experience and appreciate aesthetically pleasing objects, such as attractive arrangements of fresh flowers, textured fabrics, and the children's works of art. Learn what the children find beautiful, what they would like to add to the classroom, and how they suggest displaying special items. As you describe their work with new words and phrases, children will internalize and begin to assimilate that vocabulary in their own conversations, both in the classroom and in daily life. You might say, "You have used interesting *textures* in your collage," "I see you have colorful *patterns* in your painting," or "You have used many different *shapes* to create your sculpture." These authentic opportunities will help develop children's perceptions of the world around them through the language they learn to express their observations. Although some classrooms may not appear attractive at first glance, they can be transformed by incorporating beautiful elements. Inexpensive but effective changes like adding soft area rugs, using bamboo blinds to conceal unattractive areas, and covering the backs of old bookcases with fabrics can soften the space, add interesting textures, and provide new canvases to display children's work.

This beautifully designed environment includes a clean, warm background with variations in height, natural materials, and color, and incorporates photographs of children.

Jill's Story

Jill, a pre-K teacher, brings five tulip bulbs, a clear planter, and some smooth pebbles from her garden to her classroom. A small group of children place the pebbles in the bottom of the planter, add the bulbs, and finally pour in some water. They are excited that they will be able to watch the roots develop through the clear planter. Together, they decide that the bulbs should be placed in a sunny area of the classroom. Jill labels the arrangement *red tulip bulbs from my garden*. The children observe the developing stems and roots for several weeks, and eventually small red buds appear. Over a weekend, the tulips burst into full bloom.

On Monday, one of the children, Marie, is the first to notice the tulips on the table. Rushing to the planter, she examines the tulips intensely, smells them, and then gently rubs the petal of one tulip with her finger. She smiles broadly as she admires the beauty and soft texture of the red bloom. Several other children come to investigate and talk about the transformation in the flowers. To encourage their artistic expression, Jill adds shades of red paint to the palette in the art center. As a result, several children begin examining the flowers and painting pictures of them.

Reflection

Jill chooses to bring in tulip bulbs because she wants to share one of her interests with the children. She makes a label to encourage children's interest in print. Jill sparks the children's curiosity with the bulbs and follows their resulting interest by adding new paints that are the same colors as the tulips to the art center. In this safe and supportive environment, the children are able to touch the tulips, select the paint of their choice, and collaborate with others on their artwork.

Jill might extend the children's enthusiasm in other ways, like adding books about gardening or flower catalogs to the reading center for the children to explore. They may enjoy seeing the variety of colors and sizes flowers come in, or learning the names of flowers—even making up some of their own! These possibilities require exploring printed materials, comparing and contrasting information, making decisions, and thinking in new ways, all of which contribute to creative thinking.

Marie (age 4) is examining the features of the tulips with her teacher, Jill.

She uses red paint to represent the tulips in her artwork.

A Sense of Place

Early childhood programs are part of communities composed of diverse people, families, cultures, languages, and geographical features. Connect your classroom to the community by including materials from the local area that are familiar to the children, such as geographical elements, photographs, music, food, and stories. For instance, a school or program located in a mountainous area might showcase paintings of vegetation and wildlife that are part of the children's natural surroundings, while one located in a desert area might house a terrarium with soil, rocks, and succulent plants.

It is also important to include new elements, such as a handmade wooden puzzle, a colorful woven basket, or a rough yarn ball, that will spark children's curiosity and invite questions that lead to creative problem solving ("What is this?," "What does it do?," "Where did it come from?").

A carefully designed environment can provide the stimulus and support children need to be creative. Set up your classroom so the space encourages children's efforts to make choices, follow their ideas, and explore their interests. By blending familiar and favorite elements with novel additions, you create an intriguing classroom that challenges children to think and act in creative ways.

Diversity

Most early childhood settings include children from a variety of cultures and ethnic backgrounds, with different lifestyles, abilities, languages, religions, and family structures, all of which add richness to the setting. These differences can enhance and expand the possibilities for creative thinking and activities that are shaped by the characteristics and needs of individual children. For example, a young child who moves to music in a wheelchair may inspire others to change the way they move from place to place. A child whose family is from China and is familiar with traditional Chinese music may enjoy music that is based on a pentatonic scale (music using five notes), which offers the opportunity for the children to listen to and distinguish musical compositions from another culture. A child who was born in Belgium, raised in Africa, and is fluent in three languages may bring very different background experiences to the classroom, inspiring other children to learn about differences in language, culture, food, and customs.

A multicultural classroom display of items contributed by children and their families.

The environment—photographs, art, books, and more—should clearly reflect the diverse ethnicities, traditions, and customs of the teacher and the children who learn in that space. Intentional environments celebrate the capabilities and interests of each child and respect their important contributions to the community of learners in the classroom. When you bring in these elements, you create a place that respects the heritage and culture of the children and their families.

A corn plant is hardy and can survive in an early childhood classroom through flood or drought.

Making the Space Warm and Nurturing

Soft, translucent fabrics in light colors or with simple textures can add softness and visual interest to a space as well as coverage for materials that are not in use, eliminating distractions for children sensitive to visual stimulation (Isbell & Isbell 2008). Bolts of cloth can be draped, looped, and tied to ceilings, walls, and furnishings in interesting combinations. Sheer fabric or curtains can also be used to screen windows and storage areas or to create boundaries. These features help to provide spaces where children can slow down, think, and reflect.

In the library, group meeting areas, and other appropriate spots, arrange pillows and small blankets for children to relax on or snuggle into for warmth. Area rugs can also provide softness as well as visual interest and sound absorption. Rugs in muted colors or with simple designs are more versatile. The textures of small rugs may capture the interest of some children, and that interest can be built upon by adding yarn and weaving fabric in the art area.

Adding natural elements to the classroom, such as a nontoxic corn plant, makes the space more inviting and provides children with the opportunity to develop their observational skills and use these insights in their work. For instance, the pattern and texture of palm fronds (leaves) might intrigue a child and extend his thinking about trees or plants. He may have questions that lead to further investigation, such as "What is this?," "How do other plants look and feel?," "Can I draw this?," and "Where do they grow?"

Sounds of the Environment

Sounds can support children's creativity or distract them from their work. When creating learning centers in the classroom, group noisy areas together so they don't interfere with quiet spaces like the library or writing area. For example, block building and deconstruction are noisy activities, so the loud sounds of this area should be dampened by a rug or other sound-absorbing element. Boundaries between areas also help with acoustic insulation. A bookcase between the block and socio-dramatic play areas can be lined with thin foam or insulation and then covered with an attractive fabric. This soundproofing can also provide visual interest or function as a display space for photographs or the children's work.

Music can be used to nurture children's creativity in many ways. Use background music to excite children's enthusiasm or set the tone for an activity, such as calming music before reading a story. Providing music in an assortment of genres, rhythms, styles, volumes, and tempos will expand children's world of sounds and expose them to new musical possibilities. For example, for quiet moments, you might play Native American flute or instrumental acoustic music like cello or guitar. Marching band numbers are good for moving around the room, while traditional folk songs build connections to a particular community or culture.

You might ask the children what music they would like to hear while they are cleaning up, or what song to sing when they are gathering for a story. These choices allow the children to influence what is happening in the classroom. Help children think about the effect of the music by posing questions ("How does the music make you feel?" or "What do you like about this composition?") and talking about the different characteristics. When integrating music in the classroom, consider whether you want it to be the focus of the children's attention or unobtrusive background sound for the children's activities.

Color and Light

For many years, bright primary colors characterized the décor of almost every early childhood classroom. Influenced in part by Reggio Emilia school environments, more classrooms are moving toward light, neutral colors that can be used as a backdrop to showcase children's creative works.

The placement and amount of light in your classroom can emphasize objects in the room or signal the intended use of a space. Use light to draw attention to artwork or a creative project. Softer light can indicate that an area is a place for thinking or being quiet—a flashlight may provide all the light that is necessary. A sturdy floor lamp next to a rocker in the reading area gives enough light for reading a book, whether alone or with a friend. In the theater area, a spotlight can be used to put focus on the actors. Natural light is desirable and should be used to advantage whenever possible, while fluorescent lighting should be avoided. Dimming switches are a great tool that allow you to control and adjust the amount of light to better align with the children's activities (Isbell & Evanshen 2012). Lights can also be strategically arranged to form a place where the children can collaborate or discuss ideas in groups (Zane 2015).

The addition of a spotlight in the theater center inspires this young actress to perform.

Large and Small Groups, Partners, and Individual Work

Often, people imagine that innovative ideas come from an individual genius working in an isolated, quiet place. Although this approach does work for some, Hill and colleagues (2014) write that working together in groups to solve problems is a powerful way to identify and implement innovative ideas. A group of people can participate in the creative process by trying new ideas, making mistakes, gaining insights from each other, and ultimately generating an innovative approach.

To encourage children's innovative spirits and develop another facet of their problem-solving skills, provide them with opportunities to work, plan, implement, and reflect in a group. Group work allows children to practice working with their peers, experience different areas they can collaborate on with classmates, and gain inspiration for possible projects. It also brings together children with varied interests, social skills, and capabilities in groups where they can be successful and try new things.

Large Group or Community Meetings

Large group or community meetings can build a sense of belonging. During meeting time, young children listen to a story, sing a song, share an idea, and make plans for the day. Sometimes children hear new ideas and, inspired by the group, may talk about their creative activities and projects. Some children may be hesitant to contribute because of the large number of people in the group; others may dominate the discussions. As you lead large group meetings, guide the conversation so all children have a chance to talk. Model an appreciation for and acceptance of the children's interesting ideas, thoughtful contributions, and intriguing questions. In this setting, children develop social skills such as listening to peers, respecting ideas, and valuing unusual responses and interests.

The physical aspects of the meeting place for large group time should be conducive to focused attention and listening. It is important to create a space that has minimal distractions. Study the area carefully to eliminate any displays or items within reach, such as books or blocks, that might interfere with the children's attention.

Pose questions that will help children focus on the topic at hand, and give them sufficient time to think about the questions, respond, and elaborate on their responses. Be sure to include divergent questions (see examples on page 57) to encourage children to think in more fluent and creative ways. Plan for the day by providing various centers, activities, and experiences the children can choose from, and write down their selections. A written record helps them organize their plans, follow through, and return to the meeting space to evaluate their play, activities, and projects.

Small Groups

Small groups provide one of the most useful organizational tools for the development of creative thinking. In small groups—generally three to five children—children have more opportunities to communicate, influence the discussion of ideas, shape activities as they collaborate during the creative process, and find the materials they need to carry out their plans. Groups of this size provide a supportive environment for children to contribute ideas, formulate plans, ask questions, and adjust to the group's consensus.

Small groups need to gather in different types of physical spaces based on the objectives of their work. For example, a science experiment with magnets may work best at a table with a basket of collected materials. A small group might meet outdoors for an art project involving a gigantic piece of fabric attached to trees or a fence. Place tempera paint, paintbrushes, small spray bottles, and sponges in a portable tray on the playground close to the fabric. This outdoor space encourages large motions and the ability to splatter paint on a canvas, extending children's creative opportunities.

Small groups are especially effective in encouraging the development of the 4Cs (creativity, collaboration, communication, and critical thinking) through activities that include art, focused projects, innovations, story dramatizations, and problem solving. Groups that have fewer children foster more discussion, questions, and solutions.

Partners

For some projects and activities, having two children collaborate as partners works best. This pairing can be selected by the children, suggested by you because of a shared interest or project, or randomly assigned. Bruno (age 4) and Delanda (age 5) are both interested in the book *We're Going to the Farmers' Market* (2014), by Stefan Page. They have been talking about the market in their neighborhood, the products sold there, and what their families buy. Bruno and Delanda decide to set up their own market in the corner of the block area. They refer to the book as they decide what to sell. At first they consider selling fruits and vegetables like in the story, but ultimately they decide to sell different things. After brainstorming several possibilities, they decide to sell "pink tamales."

Sometimes partners like Bruno and Delanda have similar interests, but often, pairs are composed of children with varied interests and different capabilities. In this type of partnership, one child may be the leader or mentor while the other child is the learner. Each child gains from these interactions as they problem-solve and implement ideas.

Pairing is especially effective for a child who is uncomfortable sharing ideas in a large group. Partners can collaborate, think, and achieve results that work and are valued by both. In a pairing, each child builds confidence in his growing capabilities and creative abilities.

Individual Work

Children may prefer to work alone at times, and this choice should be respected and recognized as an appropriate way to work. The challenge is to identify a place in the busy classroom for one child to incubate an idea, focus, and persist. It may be as simple as creating a quiet area screened by large cardboard pieces or bookcases. The most important characteristic of this space is that the children recognize it as a place set aside to work on their own. When this *thinking place* is identified, children understand they can go there when they have budding ideas they want to consider alone. Donna (age 4) carries her journal into the quiet area. She is armed with a marker and several colored pencils. She reclines on the large, soft pillow and stares intently at a mobile hanging above her. For several minutes she just contemplates, not writing or drawing in her journal. This quiet area provides a place where Donna is not distracted by others and can think about the story and illustrations she wants to include in her journal.

Children also learn to recognize and respect when others are creating. You may hear children say, "Don't talk to him. He's working," "Leonardo needs quiet time to create," or "Can't you see she's thinking?" Although it is essential for young children to work together in groups, it is also necessary to recognize when a child needs to work alone and provide an area where they can do so. A thinking place is essential for a classroom that nurtures creativity and recognizes the incubation step of the creative process.

These partners are exploring how sand and balls move down an incline.

With low lights, cushions, and a couch, this area provides a quiet place for a child to think and incubate ideas.

Using Projects to Support Creativity

The project approach has been described by many, including Lilian Katz and Sylvia Chard (1999). Over a period of time, teachers and children do an in-depth study of a real-life topic children are interested in, giving children an opportunity to actively engage in deep learning about things that matter to them.

Tom Kelley and Jonathan Littman of Stanford University emphasize that in order to prepare for the age of innovation, we must be designers, problem solvers, and creators. The process of working on projects requires both thinking and tinkering (Kelley & Littman 2002).

IDEO, a global design company established by Kelley and Kelley (2013), uses a simple four-step process to design innovations and spark new ideas and possibilities. People can participate in the project design process at any age and will improve their efforts if they use the approach frequently.

Define. Focus on real-world problems. A helpful question often used by Kelley and his team is "How might we . . . ?" This identification of the problem is an important first step that helps start the project off in the right direction.

Plan. Take time to think about the elements of and constraints on the problem. If the problem involves creating or refining a product or service, questions like "How will it be used?" and "Who will use it?" must be considered. This step involves observing people and trying to understand their experiences and their needs.

Do. Use a variety of approaches to come up with a new solution or address the issue in a different way. Some techniques to use might be brainstorming, group suggestions, and individual ideas. Together, choose the most promising design and create a prototype or plan. Then test it out and document the process.

Review. Evaluate the design or plan, refine it with your findings and make changes as needed. The Do and Review phases often involve bouncing back and forth between the two steps, using information gained in the Review stage to further develop and refine the idea or product.

This process fosters creative skills and develops a deeper understand of the problem and solutions. The Partnership for 21st Century Learning (P21) (Trilling & Fadel 2009) reports that this model encourages the higher levels of motivation and engagement needed for success.

Education researcher and policy adviser Linda Darling-Hammond and colleagues (2008) reviewed the learning approaches used in a collection of research related to project learning across a span of 50 years. They concluded that there are significant benefits for students who work together on learning activities compared to students who work alone. Students working in pairs or groups exhibit greater individual and collective knowledge, higher confidence and motivation levels, and improved social interactions, including positive feelings toward other students.

In early childhood classrooms, the idea for a project may come from a group's shared interest ("Why did the petals fall off our flower?," "How do they build that very tall building?," or "How are bicycles made?"). Other times, the project focus may develop as one child demonstrates a new interest or skill. In some cases, this leads to wonderful projects where you learn and practice some of the same skills alongside of the children. For example, Naima (age 5) received a gift from her granny, a loom to make potholders. She brought it to school and worked on it in the art area during center time. The other children were fascinated by this new tool and the way Naima wove the loops of fabric to make a potholder. If you were the teacher in this classroom, what might you do to support the children's interest in this process? You don't know much about weaving, so you might ask them, "Would you like to find out how to weave? Perhaps we can discover how to weave." The problem is stated and restated in different ways, with the children deciding to pursue a project in which they learn how to weave. Naima becomes the mentor and begins to demonstrate to the interested children how to use the loops to go over and under the fabric and connect the sides. Recognizing that the children are interested in weaving, you collect other looms that can be used by children. The children then begin to work in small groups to create and share their ideas. As the project progresses, the children's skills are evolving, and they persist even when faced with obstacles. You sometimes act as a facilitator—"How do you think we might find that out?"—and at other times you provide expertise, guidance, and extensions. Later in the project, you and the children might experiment with other techniques of weaving using different materials, such as wire or natural materials, or create a huge loom that invites weaving in a very different way. During the project, the children collaborate and communicate with other teachers and experts and review what they have tried and learned. You find ways to challenge their learning and engage them at their individual levels of interest and skill.

Learning Centers That Inspire Creativity

Most learning centers encourage creative thinking because they are well-planned spaces where young children participate actively, experiment with new ideas and adapt them as needed, and practice their growing capabilities. Learning centers provide an enriched environment for nurturing the creative process, encouraging children to explore their interests by selecting a center and choosing what to do there. Gathering a small group of children in a learning center is conducive to communication, collaboration, and critical thinking. During center time, you and the children can adjust and change plans, which fosters flexible thinking and engages the children in meaningful experiences. Learning centers include a variety of objects and tools that invite children to think of possibilities and elaborate on their ideas. Perhaps some of the most important features of learning centers are that children are able to play with ideas, observe what happens, manipulate and add materials, and reflect on what they've done. This process is one of the most effective ways to stimulate creativity, foster language skills, and develop critical thinking.

Block Center

The block center has a long history of nurturing young children's exploration and creativity. Research has also identified several mathematical and scientific domains that are strengthened through construction with blocks (Chalufour & Worth 2004; Sarama & Clements 2004; Sarama & Clements 2009). Blocks offer children the means to create their own designs and express themselves. Block play encourages children to be fluent and flexible and inspires their cognitive and creative ideas.

Adding bubble wrap, wood of various sizes and shapes, pieces of fabric with interesting textures, cardboard boxes, unbreakable mirrors, and other materials that can be used in flexible ways supports children's creativity in the block center. Consider adding other items that relate to a focus in the curriculum to stimulate children's thinking. For example, if the

Teddy and William's Story

Teddy (age 5) and William (age 4) decide they are going to build an airport with four runways and a control tower. They work intently on this through the entire hour of center time. Their intricate construction unfinished, they ask their teacher if they can leave the airport set up so they can continue building it the next day. She suggests they make a sign that includes "writing" that communicates to their classmates not to touch the construction. The next day, they return to the block area with new possibilities for their airport: "How about a jumbo jet, a rescue helicopter, and small planes?" "We need a fuel truck too!" Their airport and fleet grows because they have time to develop creative ideas for expanding and developing their construction.

Reflection

The teacher has set up a well-equipped block area that includes blocks in a variety of sizes, shapes, and materials, including, wood, foam, and cardboard. During center time, she observes while Teddy and William build a complex airport and runways. She nurtures their creative ideas and supports incubation of further ideas by allowing them to keep their project intact, even suggesting that they make a sign so their classmates don't accidentally dismantle it, and giving them time to return to their project the following day. The boys' creative plan and persistent work coupled with their teacher's support leads to their completion of a detailed airport.

Two boys (age 5) and a girl (age 4) collaborate in building a spaceship with big blocks, complete with controls to make it "fly."

children are learning about birds, you might purchase inexpensive birdhouses (or build them with the children) to include in the block area. Another creative idea is to attach full-body photographs of the children on mini rectangular blocks. These blocks can enhance children's creative play and help them develop a story for their structures.

Art Center, Studio, or Atelier

The art center is an integral part of an early childhood classroom. This space often includes drawing and painting tools, easels, and tables along with a variety of materials like paper, paint, clay, cloth and paper scraps, and recycled materials. Providing traditional painting tools (like brushes and rollers) and nontraditional painting tools (like twigs and pine branches) might motivate children to paint on a huge piece of butcher paper attached to the wall. Place a plastic shower curtain on the floor to catch any drips or mess. You could display work by a famous artist to inspire the children, like a painting by well-known abstract artist Jackson Pollock, who used a "drip and splash" style by flinging paint with a stick to create rolling vortexes of color and line. Displaying three-dimensional art pieces, such as a sculpture or pottery, gives children the opportunity to touch, feel, and observe artwork from different angles. Some art centers also have a space to store children's in-progress work so they can return to refine or extend their projects.

In Reggio Emilia–inspired programs, this space for exploring, thinking, collaborating, and carrying out project work is called the *atelier*. The atelier is the center of creative activity, with children moving in and out of the area as they focus on, develop, and expand their ideas. The transformation of spaces using Reggio principles can allow creativity to blossom. Many features of the atelier can be integrated into an expanded view of the art studio; for example,

teachers can design an open, inviting place with space for group and individual work, provide a variety of easily accessible materials and tools, and visually display children's continuing projects so they can reflect on changes or additions. Equally important to the physical environment is the attitude and involvement of the adults and children as they become co-creators—posing questions, searching for possibilities, and determining what to create together. In this space, there is freedom to try something new or different and to fail. These possibilities are accepted as part of the process without focusing on the teacher's expectations or finding the "correct" solution.

The shelves in this art studio organize the materials and display them attractively.

The Value of Messing About

Messing about is a three-phase cycle developed by Frances and David Hawkins (2002):

1. Explore ideas or materials

2. Make meaning

3. Question

During the first phase, children explore materials that are open ended and free to individual interpretation. The teacher observes and attentively listens to the children. In the second phase, children identify, interpret, and define the idea or material they're exploring, aided by judicious observations and questions from the teacher that help to deepen children's investigations. A child may explore multiple possibilities in this phase. The third phase is a time for teachers and children to share ideas and reflect on the process, which may inspire new questions. This cycle, driven by children's natural curiosity, illustrates the importance of creativity in learning.

Science Center

Stock the science center with materials that intrigue and invite hands-on exploration of concepts in life science, physics, earth and space science, and chemistry. To explore physics, children can use a board to build a wide wooden incline and place objects varying in size, weight, and shape on it. As the objects go down the incline, they watch their descent, notice the differences, and wonder about those differences. Does the object roll straight down? Does it bounce, stay still, or perhaps not move at all? What would happen if children increased or decreased the slope (angle) of the incline? This experience provides children many opportunities to experiment with variables, ask questions, and make observations.

If you have an oven or a microwave in the classroom, use cooking and baking to introduce chemistry concepts. Gather the ingredients and let children experiment with measurement and mixing. Making simple recipes such as pancakes or muffins helps them learn how to manipulate variables (ingredients) and observe their transformation from liquid to solid

(and vice versa). That's chemistry! Welcome children's "mistakes" and messes just like scientists—trial and error, repetition, and problem solving are all part of the process—and enjoy the experience of learning and creating together.

Construction Center

The workshop area may include tools and materials such as screwdrivers, wooden mallets, tape measures, clamps, nuts, bolts, screws, nails, and safety goggles. Include lumber in an assortment of manageable lengths with pre-drilled holes of varying sizes, along with pieces of foam, particle board, cardboard, and sandpaper for construction projects. Provide connecting materials such as duct tape, wire, rope, and glue. These additions to the construction area foster children's creativity by providing many possibilities for creative expression and unique thinking. However, safety is extremely important: Introduce one tool at a time and safe ways to use it, and teach children a healthy respect for the tools and materials.

Fix-It or Invention Center

Nothing captures the interest of young children like things they can take apart and investigate—machines, small appliances, and other objects with movable parts. In the invention station, children can be fixers or the designers of a new innovation. For example, when Eliza (age 5) discovered an old, broken alarm clock in the fix-it center, she disassembled the clock with a screwdriver and carefully examined the inner workings. Next, she removed the gears while remembering their order. Then she oiled the gears, polished the workings, and reassembled the clock. To her surprise, the clock began ticking. Now she believes she can fix anything! Books about machines and how things work can provide additional inspiration as children determine what to build. This area sets the creative child free to select materials and have her thinking challenged in new ways.

Writing and Illustrating Center

Children communicate their ideas through drawing and writing, and this area, specifically designed for children to record their thoughts and ideas using symbols (letters, child-created marks, etc.), provides the tools that fit their level of fine motor coordination. This can include markers, crayons, paintbrushes, chalk, scissors, magnetic letters, colored pencils, clay tools, and trays to work on. Add a selection of paper, including child-crafted books, notebooks, chart paper, colored construction paper, computer paper, butcher paper, and parchment paper. Use folders, portfolios, and boxes to organize their work and encourage persistence on their writing and illustrating. Some children may want to record their ideas and stories to express or organize their thinking. Others may find that dictating their ideas and stories to the teacher is a more effective way to keep their creative flow going.

Theater Center

Children sometimes get inspired when listening to a story and want to act it out. A theater area provides the perfect place to nurture developing thespians. Some children may want to write and produce their own play. The process of acting out a story or writing and producing an original play can develop over several weeks and involve identifying the theme or plot, determining the character parts, setting up the stage and props, and ultimately presenting the play to a live audience. This project is a wonderful integrated learning experience. Some questions or problems that the children should identify and address include these:

> What will the production be about?

> Who are the characters, and what will they do? Who will play each character?

> What is the sequence of events?

> Do we need costumes?

> Can we involve the audience?

> Would our families or other classes like to see it?

During this process, children develop their oral language skills, expand their vocabulary, and use their imagination and critical thinking skills by tackling challenges: "Who is directing this production?," "We need to have tickets," and "Are we selling refreshments?" Children also learn how stories work—they have a setting, a message, and a sequence with a beginning, middle, and ending. Children design and construct the necessary stage, props, or costumes. By speaking before an audience, extemporaneously responding to others, and enjoying the appreciation of their peers, they gain confidence in their ability to come up with complex ideas and act on them.

Music Center

Music offers children numerous creative opportunities. Provide music from different cultures and genres, and incorporate songs throughout the day to increase children's awareness of and interest in music. For example, play a drum while you are telling children a story, sing with children during group time, or play soft, instrumental music during snack time. Share a story about your own music experience, such as your favorite song or your first concert attendance, and listen to

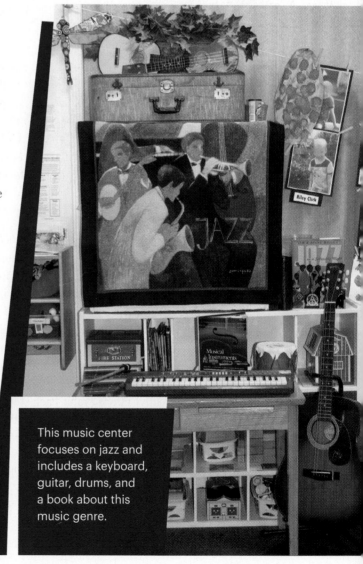

This music center focuses on jazz and includes a keyboard, guitar, drums, and a book about this music genre.

their stories and experiences as well. Wonder with children how music instruments are made and why some instruments sound a certain way. Bring an instrument to the classroom for children to explore and play. A broken instrument offers an excellent opportunity for children to experiment with sounds and even repair!

Add materials to the music center that reflect the children's interests. Do they enjoy imitating or listening to a famous singer? If so, provide a stage and props for performances. Are they composing their own music using the unit blocks or pots and pans from the other centers and turning them into a drum set? Provide a variety of drums or hang metal measuring cups to strike with metal spoons or mallets. Are they interested in creating a guitar-like string instrument using a cardboard box and some rubber bands? Prepare a working space with some recycled materials and assist them with resources and planning. Perhaps they're interested in an orchestra with various types of musical instruments. Organize the music center with visual materials such as books about an orchestra, posters of a famous maestro, or recordings of classical performances and headsets. Watch a video clip from a concert with the class. However you set it up, the music center should nurture budding musicians' inner musicality and interests, introducing them to new instruments and activities.

The Importance of the Creative Arts

During the early years, the creative arts can provide children with new opportunities, build on existing interests, and expand their life experiences. You can integrate the arts into the curriculum, providing open-ended experiences that allow children of varying abilities and interests to be successful. Posner and Patoine (2009) suggest that the arts encourage brain development and strengthen cognition. Art, music, movement, and drama activities elicit focused attention, which shapes and sculpts brain networks.

Gardner's (2011) work has helped explain that children "know the world" through different combinations of several intelligences. The arts particularly support children who have strengths in the musical, bodily-kinesthetic, spatial, interpersonal, and intrapersonal intelligences. The visual and performing arts fulfill some of children's emotional needs, such as allowing them to express their feelings, use their ideas, collaborate, and solve disagreements. Both children and adults need to develop a sense of self-worth. Young children are just beginning to learn about the world and their individual capabilities. They may fail or make mistakes, and sometimes they get frustrated; in these instances, children need adults who appreciate their creative efforts, value each step, and provide time, materials, and support for the messy process of discovering. Since there is no exact way to paint a picture, or a right or wrong way to retell a story, the artistic process offers a safe way for young children to try out possibilities, experiment with materials, and learn about themselves (Edwards 2010). The arts support creativity, learning, and the whole child.

Chris (age 5) is learning about the properties of clay as he shapes and rolls the material.

Visual Arts

Art is an essential component of a quality early childhood program. When art experiences are designed effectively, children develop artistic abilities and gain an appreciation for beauty in their world. Art is recognized as a fundamental, distinctive knowledge that helps children represent their world, thoughts, and feelings. Through art, children are powerful. They are able to freely express their feelings by using colors, patterns, and brushstrokes; combining materials; and designing three-dimensional projects (clay, wire sculpture, or natural materials). Since many art materials are open ended, children can plan how to use them, follow through with action, and create amazing work. They examine new methods, sharpen their observation skills, use novel tools that extend their creative thinking, and participate in detailed projects. As children work with a broader range of media and are supported by thoughtful, responsive teachers, they become more skilled—able to imagine and create more complex works.

Young children progress through a predictable pattern of artistic development, from uncontrolled scribble to controlled scribble. During the preschool years, many children begin to use basic forms in their drawings and organize shapes on the page. They gain better control over tools like paintbrushes, crayons, scissors,

Creating an Environment That Nurtures Artistic Creativity

As a teacher, your role is to enrich children's artistic experiences by

› Providing time and space for pursuing creative endeavors

› Emphasizing the process rather than a product

› Recognizing that children need to explore materials and tools in their own ways

› Developing a climate of acceptance

› Displaying children's work they wish to share

› Encouraging self-evaluation

› Including a treasure box of unique items for exploration and inspiration

› Incorporating individual, partner, and small group creative opportunities

› Providing storage for in-process projects and revisiting work

The Progression...

Noticing and incorporating increasing details in our paintings and drawings.

Flowers have special characteristics that are unique.

Lucy's (age 5) painting on the left was done in the fall of her first year in a pre-K program. The painting in the center shows her work the following spring, a result of experience, observing others' artwork (such as shown on the right), and using different techniques and tools. The later painting has more details and shows an expanded understanding of overall composition.

markers, and chalk. Around 4 to 7 years old, children enter the representational art stage, meaning they progress from using basic forms to producing symbols that represent objects in their world. Although these stages are predictable, there are variations among children of the same chronological age or developmental stage. Many of these differences are influenced by a child's experiences, opportunities, and interests.

Art education experiences introduce children to the amazing world of art, teaching them to appreciate works of art and introducing them to artists they can study as models of the creative process. Young children can appreciate Renoir's *Child with Toys*, a painting of a mother and child playing, or be intrigued by the symbolic painting of a young boy and animals in Goya's *Manuel Osorio Manrique de Zuñiga*. Draw children's attention to a new work of art and discuss the content, color, design, or specific subjects. For *Child with Toys*, you might say, "Let's look at the toys Renoir included in this painting. How are they different or similar to the toys you have?," "If you were painting your toys, what might you include?," "What do you like about this painting?," and "What do you notice about the colors Renoir used?"

Music Possibilities for Young Children

Music is an audible form of art. Children have a natural interest in sound; they are exposed to rhythmic patterns, environmental noises, and vocalizations even before birth. Encouraging children to experience music in an early childhood program contributes significant benefits to a child's overall development, serving their emotional, intellectual, social, and creative needs (Kelley & Sutton-Smith 1987; NAfME 2016; Rauscher et al. 1997).

Many teachers experience anxiety when they think about providing music activities for children, believing they have little musical talent or that teaching music belongs to professional musicians. But music in early childhood programs does not have to be taught by a professional, just as painting does not have to be taught by an artist. Watch an infant discover and explore sound and rhythm as she strikes two blocks together repeatedly, or a toddler who places his mouth on the open end of a small plastic container and says "Ahh!" Did the infant replace the block with another material, like a rattle, or strike different surfaces to explore different sounds? How about the toddler? Did the child say "Ahh!" again softly and then loudly? Observe a preschooler sing while he selects a costume in the dramatic play area. Did the child sing faster, slower, or off-beat, or perhaps add some original words to the song? Participate with children as they make rhythms, especially when they are exploring an instrument or object that generates the sound. Do a call and response activity with children so they can experience the difference in rhythm and the continuity of patterns; for example, a child beats the drum twice, you respond by beating twice, then vary the rhythm as you continue. Sing along with a child, even if you don't know the song or melody he is using, and make up a song together with and without words. Sing fast or slow, loud or soft. And remember, children are unconcerned with the quality of your singing!

Children enjoy exploring and varying the components of sound, such as volume, pitch, duration, and timbre (Goldstein 2014). As you explore instruments or voices together, ask questions that help children focus on these components: "Can you beat the drum louder?" (volume); "Can you sing with your high voice?" (pitch); "Let's see how long we can hum together!" (duration); "Can you make the same sound Amelie is making?" (timbre).

If you are reading a story that talks about sound, remark on it: "What do you think the 'wind's whistle' was like? Let's try out some different ways it might sound." Children will enjoy the challenge and come up with ideas on their own.

Introduce music to children through the contexts of music appreciation (listening), music performance (singing and playing instruments), and music creation (improvising or composing songs and creating musical instruments). To expand children's musical appreciation, provide them with both familiar and unfamiliar music. Many early childhood programs play recordings of children's songs with lyrics, but be sure to also play instrumental pieces, such as a piano solo or a jazz ensemble. Create a collection that spans many music genres—classical (solo, ensemble, or orchestra), music from different cultures and countries, contemporary music performed with unusual instruments, and music from popular plays. Select music based on different tonality, like sad or contemplative music (slow music played in a minor key, for example) and cheerful music (upbeat music played in a major key). A rich variety of music enables children to identify their own musical interests and stimulates creative thinking.

Creative Movement/Dance

As children mature, they gain better control and coordination of their bodies and learn different ways of moving. Creative movement activities let children respond to open-ended experiences in their own way, express their thoughts and emotions, and build confidence in their physical and expressive capabilities.

One of the intelligences identified in Gardner's (2011) multiple intelligences is bodily-kinesthetic. This relates to being able to combine the body and mind in a physical activity. Though movement is important for all children, for some it is the way they "solve problems or create" (Pica 2013). Unfortunately, motor activity often is given limited time in preschool and elementary settings. Creative movement opportunities should emphasize children's satisfaction and enjoyment in expressing themselves with their bodies and in participating with others.

Pica (2013) describes two child-centered approaches to providing experiences that encourage motor development and creative movement. *Guided discovery* is a convergent problem-solving approach that encourages some experimentation and inventiveness. A teacher might select and guide a song or an activity and encourage the children to discover different ways to use their bodies. For example, the traditional folk song "The Animal Fair" provides an opportunity for children to move like the animals identified. Try asking questions like "How do birds and beasts arrive at the fair?" or "How does the big baboon walk?"

Exploration, a divergent problem-solving approach to movement activities, best supports the development of creative thinking. This approach invites children to choose their own response to a challenge, determine how they will move, and evaluate their choice. For example, say to the children, "How can you move two parts of your body at the same time?," "How are the two parts of your body working together?," "Show me how you can move two

Writing his composition on staff paper helps Ja'von (age 5) represent his musical thinking.

other parts of your body," and "How did that combination work?" When questions and challenges like these are combined with music, you'll encourage even more experimentation.

Movement activities, including dancing and walking, provide a break from intensive cognitive activity or a demanding project. Taking time to move will inspire new thinking and ideas when a child is stuck or unable to find a solution (Sawyer 2013).

Creative Drama/Theater

Creative drama is a wonderful way for young children to express their ideas and improvise while developing their creative thinking. Some appealing possibilities include pantomime, group drama, literature enactment, socio-dramatic play, and puppetry, all of which enable children to find solutions to issues through dramatization. In each of these areas of the dramatic arts, children determine their own actions, dialogue, sound effects, and props. The focus is not on performance or perfection but on the process and development of the drama. Creative drama supports children's communication, conflict resolution, and decision-making skills.

Enacting Children's Stories

The first step in story enactment is selecting an engaging story to read, like *The Gigantic Turnip* (2009), by Aleksey Nikolayevich Tolstoy and Niamh Sharkey. Stories work best for dramatization if they contain a simple story line, three to five characters, repetitive phrases or words, and an ending with a clear resolution. Before reading the story, ask questions to help the children listen for specific content, and after reading, return to those questions to determine what the children remember. Ask the children an open-ended question, such as "What character would you like to be in the story and why?"

A few days later, reread the story, discuss the characters and sequence of events, and guide the children to think about acting out the story. Have them select the characters they want to play—one may want to be the main character, the grandfather, while another might want to be the tiny bird. A child who prefers not to participate in the acting can be part of the audience. Later, if he feels more confident, he can be part of the drama.

Although no props are needed to dramatize a story, children may make suggestions; for instance, one child might say that the boy planting the turnip seed needs a hat because he will be in the sun. In their character roles, the children use their own words and dramatize the story without rehearsal. During the action they adjust and adapt to the words spoken by others, which requires creative thinking. These extemporaneous responses can lead to some interesting versions of the story. After the drama is complete, talk with children about their experience, both what they liked and what could be done differently. To help the children see things from a different perspective, they can trade roles to reenact the story several more times. Encourage children to reflect on the different interpretations they are making. How do different actors change the story or tone?

An effectively designed early childhood environment provides a safe place where children and their often surprising ideas are respected and valued. It provides the space and options that enable children to work together or incubate ideas individually. There is a balance between familiar, loved areas and new possibilities that touch on their interests and challenge their thinking. It is an aesthetically pleasing environment, not because of expensive items but because of the beautiful objects, paintings, and children's creations that are carefully selected and displayed attractively. Children need an interesting, thought-provoking, and supportive space for creativity to flourish.

Reflections

> Examine your community meeting (large group) space. What does it communicate to children? Are there distractions that might keep them from fully engaging in group activities? What can you change?

> When do children have the opportunity to work in small groups? What are they doing during this time? What could you do to foster deeper thinking, exploration, and collaboration during small group times?

> Do you have an area where a child can work alone or have a quiet place to think and incubate ideas? If not, how could you create a place for quiet thinking?

> How might you develop and share new centers with other teachers to increase the children's options for play and discovery?

> How do you exhibit the children's (and your own) creativity?

> Which learning centers in your room seem to stimulate children's most innovative thinking? Are there other centers that could encourage children to play with ideas and collaborate on possibilities? What new areas might you add to make the environment more nurturing of creative thinking and problem solving?

> Which of the arts are available to the children throughout the week? How can you incorporate other opportunities?

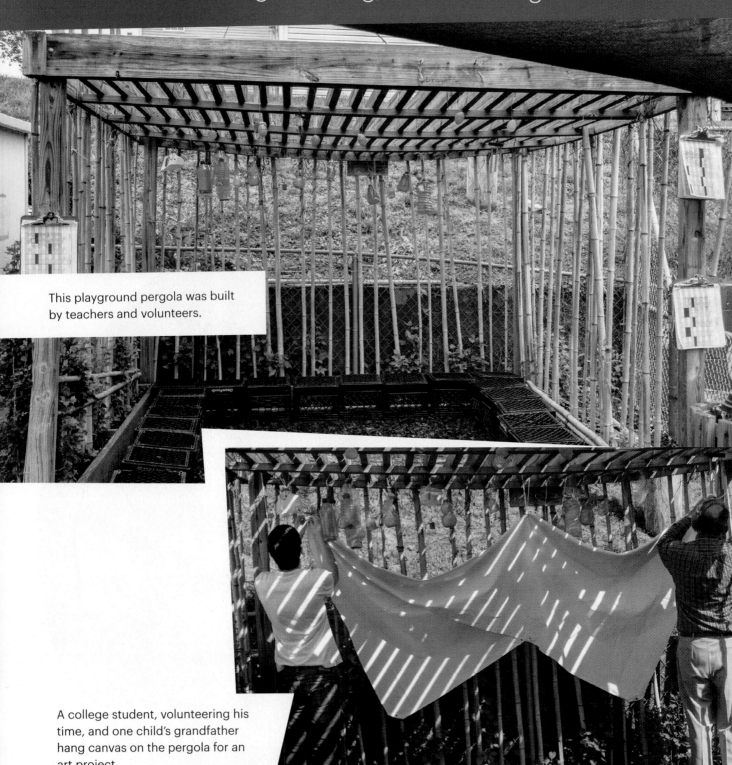

This playground pergola was built by teachers and volunteers.

A college student, volunteering his time, and one child's grandfather hang canvas on the pergola for an art project.

Edwel (age 3) adds some final touches to completely cover the canvas with yellow paint, creating a poem as he synchronizes his words with the movement of this paintbrush.

"All yellow . . . all yellow . . . here and here, there and there . . ."

, the teacher, helps one of the artists
up with a large, donated shirt
e painting the canvas. "I am going
ake something BIG!" the child says.
you will," says Elena, "but let's put
BIG shirt on you first!" "Ooh, I can't
I have lots of BIG ideas!"

Ben (age 4) is splattering black paint and creating a new design.

"I am signing my name . . . then another sign here . . . it has to be long, up here . . . there!"

These boys (age 3) add red paint to the canvas.

"This is a BIG FIRE!"

Chapter 4

Characteristics of Creative Children and Adults

Children and adults need both a sense of belonging and to be aware of themselves as separate, creative individuals.

—Tina Bruce, *Cultivating Creativity: For Babies, Toddlers and Young Children, Second Edition*

To better understand creativity, researchers have studied its four dimensions (the creative person, the creative process, the environment, and the product), noted in Chapter 2. As an early childhood teacher, you have the opportunity to observe a creative person—the young child. Children's behaviors are often used to illustrate the characteristics of creative thinkers—characteristics that also apply to creative adults (Isbell & Raines 2013). So what are these characteristics? In what ways do children exhibit creativity? How does creativity change over time?

Characteristics of Creative Young Children

Torrance (1962) describes young children as the most creative people in the world. In Table 4.1, some of the characteristics of young children that led Torrance to this conclusion are shown alongside the characteristics typically observed in creative adults. Torrance used these similarities in his research to explain the amazing abilities of young children, and his work remains a stellar contribution to the field.

Table 4.1. Characteristics of Young Children and Creative Adults

Young Children	Creative Adults
Curious	Curious
Independent	Independent thinkers
Playful	Play with possibilities
Adventurous	Try new things
Active participants	Do rather than watch
Imaginative	Vivid imaginations
Uninhibited	Not limited by conventions

Curiosity

As any parent or teacher knows, children are curious! It has been estimated that a child asks more than one hundred questions each day (Bronson & Merryman 2010). They explore their environment in planned and unplanned ways—they might examine the dirt they used to plant a flower or flush a toilet over and over to watch the water swirl. They are interested in understanding how things work, enjoy taking things apart (even if they can't quite get them back together), and are driven to find answers to their questions.

John's Story

John (age 4) has been in the bathroom for a long time. Concerned, his teacher goes to check on him. To her amazement she finds John standing in a puddle of water in front of the bathroom sink. "What are you doing?" she asks. Excited, John explains that he has been experimenting. "First I wet a paper towel and stuffed it up the faucet. Then I turned on the water as hard as I could with both hands and watched where it went!" The teacher looks around the bathroom and realizes that this experiment has been going on for some time. Soggy paper towel pieces are stuck to the ceiling, the wall, and all over the floor.

Story Reflection

At this moment, the teacher is probably not thinking, "What a creative boy John is!" But consider John's process, which certainly displays his curiosity and ingenuity. He has several questions he wants to find an answer to: "How can I make this paper towel fly through the air?," "How far will it go?," and "Does turning the handles in different ways affect the distance the paper towel goes?" He designs an experiment to figure out the answers by manipulating objects (the paper towel and the faucet) and variables (using varying amounts of water pressure). Through his problem-solving process, John answers his questions and learns quite a bit about physics. The evidence is clearly visible all over the bathroom!

Independence

Most young children want to make their own decisions and accomplish things *their* way. They mix the paint colors *they* choose, select the clothing *they* want to wear, and select the book *they* want to read. This developing independence is a quality to be valued and supported in the early childhood classroom. Thinking and reflecting autonomously enables children to experiment with ideas that lead to creative solutions. In contrast, children who are used to others making decisions and doing things for them may need encouragement and structured opportunities to think and act on their own. Provide these children limited choices in simple, small decisions so they can become more confident in taking the initiative for learning.

Playfulness

Play is a critical element that impacts how children learn and the opportunities they have to be creative. Throughout the day, young children may play with blocks, pretend to be a race car driver, and generate ideas—"Maybe the guinea pig would like a jacket!" As they play, children are continually using their imagination to think in new, exciting ways. A hero wearing a blue cape to fly in the classroom may suddenly transform into a giant dinosaur looking for a friend. During play, children can laugh, examine possibilities and test hypotheses, and talk about and adapt their experiences to begin to understand how the world works (Brown & Vaughan 2010). Play offers a path to creative ideas as children discover how to express themselves. As children move into adulthood, the benefits they gain and the lessons they learn from play follow them, extending their ability to think creatively and problem-solve.

The girls create an imaginative story line about animals going shopping with their families as they arrange miniature animals in their "pretend mall."

Dina's Class's Story

Declan (age 5) has just returned from his family's vacation in Hawaii with pictures and shells to share with the other children in Dina's class. He has a big idea to create a beach with his friends in the dramatic area. Inspired by his vacation story, all the children want to participate in creating a beach center. "We need to bring water!" Aricia (age 5) shouts. Dawn (age 5) says, "I want to wear a rainbow skirt like hula dancers!" and she stands up and starts dancing. "I want to swim in the blue ocean and find more shells!" Declan says. With all of these exciting play ideas from the children, Dina asks them what they need to do to transform their space into a beach. As a substitute for ocean water, they brainstorm about painting the floor with blue paint, spreading a blue tarp, or gluing blue construction paper together. The blue tarp sounds like a good possibility, so Miriam (age 5) volunteers to ask her dad to bring one to class.

The next challenge is the hula costume. Dawn says she wants to make a skirt out of colorful ribbons, but she does not have lots of ribbons at home or at school. Wilma (age 5) suggests that she can make one from colorful construction paper. Suddenly Marsha (age 5) remembers her recent birthday party decorations and shouts, "Paper ribbons! We could use the soft, colorful ones!" She is referring to crepe streamers, which Dina happens to have in abundance in her classroom. During the week, the children play as swimmers; hula dancers, some of whom even blow fire (made of yellow streamers) from their mouths; and surfers holding a surfboard made out of painted recycled cardboard.

Story Reflection

One child's experiences sometimes inspire collaborative play that is rich with creative possibilities. In this story, the children's play centers not on materials prepared by the teacher but on props and materials suggested by the children as they work together. The teacher becomes the facilitator, acknowledging children's ideas and guiding them to workable solutions (using a tarp to represent the ocean) instead of ones that are impractical (painting the floor blue). As they repeat this process of trial and error and problem solving, the children adapt their ideas to accomplish their mutual goal and extend their play ideas. Their involvement in the development of the beach center provides them with many opportunities to be creative.

Summer's Story

Summer is a 5-year-old with Down syndrome. Today she is painting at an easel. On the top shelf of her easel, there are brushes and paints in clear jars. Summer decides to paint a horse using brown paint and the largest brush. This is her first time painting a horse, and she proceeds to outline an enormous figure on the paper with her paintbrush. The shape has a huge body, four legs, and two pointed ears. Summer stands back and looks at the developing picture and then colors the inside of the shape a rich brown. After the horse is painted to her satisfaction, she paints two large black eyes on the head. She smiles at her masterpiece, walks around to see other children's pictures, and returns several times to admire her work.

Story Reflection

Summer is an adventurous child who is willing to try new materials and experiences. She has a good understanding of what a horse looks like, including its color and shape. During the process of painting, she selects and uses new tools, such as a large paintbrush and tempera paint. She is confident in her ability to paint the horse, does not ask for assistance, and is immensely pleased with her results. She does not ask the teacher for approval but makes her own evaluation and is personally satisfied with her efforts.

Adventurous

Creative adults tend to be adventurous, and most young children are too. Ready and willing to try new things, they are confident in their success and aren't deterred by what others think of their ideas. This trait allows children to explore without concern about what the final product will be. An adventurous spirit empowers children to explore new materials, combine items in unique ways, and take risks that may lead to failure—or to a better idea!

Active Participants

Young children learn best and are able to extend their thinking when they are actively involved in what they are doing. They want to *do* rather than listen to directions on how to do an activity. (Even when children listen, many do the activity in the way they want and use the materials in different—often interesting!—ways.) Children who are told that mixing red and blue together results in purple gain a better understanding of color if they actually mix the paint colors themselves and observe the effect. A teacher reading a story about a tall tree to the group may inspire some children to jump high and actively experience how "tall" feels. This active participation engages learners and sustains their involvement in experiences. It also gives them opportunities to solve problems, whether it's what to do when there's no more green paint to finish their space capsule, or how to prop up the sagging trellis for the beans growing in the class garden.

Manuela (age 4) is searching for the rocks she wants to sort and classify.

Imaginative

You can see children's imaginations at work when they transform stones into cookies and later, when those same stones become eyes on their nature collage. They can pretend to be a parent taking care of a baby and play the part of the baby at the same time. When you observe children's play and see their use of symbolic representation, you gain insight into how they think and how flexible they can be. Providing rich experiences and a variety of books is essential for the development of imagination, and engaging activities encourage children to explore ideas and materials. Children try out new roles and ideas, revisit activities, and express their understanding of the way things work (Korn-Bursztyn 2012).

Lee (age 4) tries to make eyes for this clay figure by poking holes in the clay with his fingers. After a while, he decides to use additional soft clay to create two round balls for the eyes.

A Restaurant Center's Story

A new restaurant center is set up in the classroom, and four children choose to play in this area. After some discussion they decide to create a Mexican restaurant. They excitedly begin decorating the table and chairs in the center with brightly colored fabrics and use large sheets of paper to create colorful decorations on the wall. Maria (age 4) tells the others, "We need menus to know what to eat." Mandela (age 5) and Dorothea (age 5) proceed to create menus. They staple several pages of orange paper together and use markers to draw pictures and add a price of one dollar to each of the items that will be available (tacos, enchiladas, chips, and drinks). Freddie (age 4) decides he wants to be the waiter. "I will tell them where to sit. I need paper and a pencil." They return to their play the next day and again assume their roles of customer, waiter, cashier, and cook.

Story Reflection

The children draw on their imaginations to decorate their restaurant with colorful fabrics, create menus, and determine the specific roles needed in the restaurant setting. They expand their language when they use new vocabulary to describe the Mexican food and role-play as the restaurant staff. This play offers plenty of opportunities for interacting, collaborating, and making decisions.

Lack of Inhibition

As previously mentioned, most young children are unconcerned with what others think of their work. This allows them the freedom to generate ideas without worrying how their efforts will be viewed or evaluated by others. Kelley and Kelley (2013), Lehrer (2012), and Runco (2014) are just a few of the many writers who suggest that there are a multitude of benefits to being childlike, freeing the creative thinker from perceived restraints and encouraging the flow of unconventional ideas.

Children sometimes show little interest in displaying their work or taking it home. The process was what was important to them; after their work is finished, they do not need to have it admired by others. When a creation is special to a child, he may be more interested in showing it off. Before you display something a child has created, ask if he wants it displayed. If he has several creations, find out how he views them: "Is there one you would like to put on our display board?" and "What is special to you about this one?" This gives the child a voice for his preference and the opportunity to decide if others should see this particular project. The child's description of the work, the choices he made while creating it, and how he evaluates it will provide the teacher with new insight into his thinking.

Not all children will possess all of these qualities, but recognizing these attributes as part of creativity will help you identify and support children's efforts. Although some characteristics children display—constantly asking questions, using materials in unforeseen ways, and being more absorbed by the process of creating than in a final product—may frustrate adults, they often are the very elements that make creative thinkers.

Seeing Creativity in All Children

Most early childhood classrooms include children with a wide range of abilities and needs. It is important to recognize that creativity is not limited to a few children who show unusual talent in a particular area. One child may enjoy composing songs in the bathroom stall, another might be adept at offering just the right type of comfort to a distressed peer, and another may continually try things, fail, and try a different way to accomplish the task. Children with complex needs or learning difficulties can be extremely creative and bring enriching ideas into the classroom. By providing time and plenty of choices, you can support children's individual interests and creative ideas. In a supportive inclusive environment, children create together, share possibilities, and benefit from collaborative interactions and projects.

Individual Interests

Children have their own interests that are formed by their personal experiences inside and outside the early childhood setting, materials they have used, family interactions, their cultural backgrounds, and a number of other factors. These influences nurture a child's creative development. A child may show interest and aptitude in music, drawing and painting, organization, mathematics, social interaction, or fluency of ideas and persistence. A child who comes from a home filled with music will often demonstrate a deep interest in or familiarity with music, while a child whose family camps and hikes may be drawn to investigate natural materials, such as the leaves and insects on the playground. If a child has a parent who is a potter, she may choose to use a variety of clay tools and exercise advanced techniques in the art center. A child who is skilled or knowledgeable in a certain area may also mentor others by scaffolding their understanding with conversations, demonstrations, and collaboration on projects related to their interests.

As you observe children and notice their interests and related skills, you gain insight into ways to support them in the classroom with materials, experiences, and other resources. Sometimes a child's interest may be short-lived, but at other times the interest continues for a long period of time. Encouraging the interests of a child or a small group of children will support their engagement in the creative process, enabling them to come up with additional ideas to explore, materials to combine, and so on. When children are interested and engaged, they are more persistent on a project or idea. Talk to families to see what they notice their children involved in at home; find out what excites each child.

Some children have unique interests in a specialized area. One child may be deeply interested in frogs and their habitat, another in how analog clocks function. Value and nurture these fascinations, for they may be the avenues through which these children learn best and accomplish the most. Sometimes other children also become fascinated by such interests, offering the child who is exploring a unique topic a chance to share her knowledge and be an "expert."

Children With Diverse Abilities

In your setting you may have children with special needs, such as language delays, physical or visual impairments, or autism spectrum disorder (ASD). It is important to remember that *all* children can imagine and invent, and supporting those abilities is crucial. For example, Timothy, a child with autism, is drawn to a collection of small connecting blocks displayed on a large, low table in his classroom. He uses all of the blocks to construct a complex, multilayered structure that spreads over the entire table. His teacher observes his interest in blocks and sits beside him. She uses some blocks herself and verbally describes what Timothy is doing. His persistence is demonstrated as he works for a significant amount of time on the intricate structure. His interest in the blocks and his focus on building a complex structure for a long period of time reveal strengths in constructing and concentration. Over time, his teacher adds other toys to the block display to encourage him to try various combinations of different materials. Timothy's creations also inspire other children to try some of his techniques and venture into new ways of constructing. His teacher builds on this curiosity by setting up the area so other children can explore building together. A child's interest, whatever it may be, can illuminate the path to success and joy in learning.

Jeffrey (age 5) has a physical disability and is unable to use his hands to paint; however, he tells wonderful stories filled with descriptive language, sound effects, and powerful characters. His extensive language skills and storytelling ability are talents that his teacher urges him to use in a variety of activities, such as describing science experiments and spinning original stories. The other children also enjoy Jeffrey's storytelling, which affirms and encourages his efforts. Recognizing a child's strengths and capabilities is especially imperative when working with children with special needs, but is valuable for all children. In an environment designed to encourage participation and creativity, we celebrate and appreciate all children's gifts and interests.

(Top) In this sand tray, there are many options for Matthew (age 5) to include in his play.

(Bottom) Matthew is reflecting on the sand he used and recording his experience in his personal journal.

Kory's Story

A consistent classroom routine is very important to Kory (age 5), who has ASD. He always arrives at his kindergarten classroom on time, places his backpack in his cubby with the straps facing up, and fixes his shirt collar before he runs to the terrarium to see Henry, the class's pet turtle. Kory usually observes Henry for about five minutes before he joins his classmates on the rug, but today he continues to sit beside the terrarium, looking very serious and holding a pencil and a piece of paper. His teacher says, "Kory, why don't you join your friends?" His friend Lisa shouts, "Kory, here!" and taps his spot on the rug. He does not respond, instead drawing on the paper he is holding. Then he tears the paper carefully with his fingers.

After several minutes, Kory's teacher signals her assistant teacher, Maggie, to approach Kory. Kory screams, "No! Not yet!" Maggie says kindly, "Kory, it is time for you to join your friends." "No!" he insists.

Kory pushes Maggie away and several pieces of paper fall to the floor. He frantically picks up the pieces while Maggie observes quietly, allowing him to retrieve the pieces and calm himself. Catching a glimpse of some of the pieces, she sees smiling faces, a turtle's foot, and the back of a turtle shell with the tail sticking out. "Kory, are you drawing Henry?" she asks.

Kory shouts, "Tape!" He runs to get the tape from the art shelf, cuts it into short pieces, and sticks some tape on each piece of paper. He carefully sticks each paper inside the terrarium around Henry and says, "Friend." When Maggie, puzzled, lowers her body to see the terrarium from Kory's perspective, she smiles. She sees many paper turtle friends, created by Kory, smiling and waving at Henry inside the terrarium. Now that Henry isn't alone anymore, Kory moves to the carpet to sit with his friends.

Story Reflection

Kory enjoys drawing animals and insects with expressions and details and from different angles and perspectives. In this inclusive classroom, the assistant teacher's support enables Kory to follow his interests. Because Maggie gives Kory time and space to visit the turtle as part of his routine every morning, he has come to think of Henry as a friend. Noticing Henry was isolated, Kory believed that Henry needed friends, which he could draw for Henry. If Kory had been forced to abandon this venture and join the other children for group time, his teachers would have missed the opportunity to discover Kory's empathy and creative inspiration that benefited his turtle friend.

It is essential to recognize that children have different, creative perspectives, coming from a variety of backgrounds, cultures, languages, interests, abilities, and beliefs. Their past experiences distinctively shape their choices—the ways they exercise their independence and work with other children, express their ideas, solve problems, and find joy in being adventurous. Each child needs opportunities that support and extend her thinking while building her confidence. And each needs something else—a teacher who is sensitive to children's needs and interests and encourages creative exploration, and who recognizes and nurtures her own creative abilities.

Creative Teachers

It is important to distinguish between creative teaching and teaching for the development of creativity in children (Craft 2002). As a creative teacher, you might

> Plan activities using engaging approaches or materials

> Work around unusual features of your classroom space to create a supportive learning environment

> Display the children's writing in attractive arrangements that highlight their efforts

> Integrate music into the day by using a familiar melody and substituting words to fit the current classroom activity

> Add a cooking area to explore the process of transformation (chemistry) when you notice children losing interest in the life science area

These examples model creative thinking for children as you try new approaches, show you are willing to learn from mistakes, and persist until you are satisfied with the outcome. Children also benefit from hearing you verbalize your thinking process; for example, saying phrases like "I noticed that several of you have been writing some great stories lately, so I thought about what we could do to share them with other people who would enjoy them. Here are a couple of my ideas . . . ," "I am thinking about other possibilities for . . . ," or "This didn't work out like I thought it would, so I decided to . . . " helps children better understand how to think through possibilities and solutions. Observing their teacher exhibit creative behavior and use accompanying language inspires children to think in different ways and try new approaches themselves.

Creative teachers exhibit many traits that support the development of children's creativity, including playfulness, an attitude of trust toward children, and the ability to provide an emotionally supportive atmosphere

Playfulness

One of the most important characteristics of creative early childhood teachers is playfulness. Creative teachers play with possibilities, experiment with different materials, and provide engaging activities and experiences that pique children's interest and curiosity. Interactions with children are often unpredictable and changeable. This requires teachers to contemplate, think quickly, adjust, revisit conversations, and extend experiences. Creative teachers are comfortable with temporary ambiguity or confusion, enjoy watching how a project evolves, and are able to adjust to changing circumstances (Isbell & Raines 2013; Sluss & Jarrett 2007; Tegano, Groves, & Catron 1999). They also encourage divergent thinking and messy experiences because they understand the importance of playing with possibilities

This stage in the theater center—an elevated space with props and stage lighting—inspires children to present their stories, dramatize, or perform in front of others. The stage features a microphone, spotlights, and musical instruments. The children also use instruments made from shaped, thick poster boards with attached pictures of a banjo, bass, and violin. Influenced by their local musical traditions, children enjoy pretending to be bluegrass musicians.

while developing ideas. Teachers who understand the value of creative thinking devise opportunities where children can participate in open-ended play activities, experiment with novel materials, and generate multiple possibilities when problem solving (Isbell & Raines 2013). Because they understand the joy of creating and learning, they actively seek to instill that same joy in children.

Trust

The creative teacher recognizes and values that children express creativity in many ways and are brimming with ideas; therefore, she trusts that children will have interesting suggestions, work out solutions to difficult problems, have individual interests, and collaborate with each other. Understanding the capabilities of children, she supports their emerging abilities and extends their creative activities. This trust builds children's confidence in their abilities as they learn and develop. A flexible teacher provides choices so children can shape their participation and follow their interests, but she also understands that guidance or cues are sometimes needed. Asking open-ended questions that prompt children to share their ideas or offering challenges they are capable of solving reinforces children's confidence in their thinking and learning skills. As children become more independent learners, they need opportunities to choose activities, centers, materials, work and play partners, and techniques for accomplishing tasks. When children see that they have their teacher's support and trust, it encourages and unlocks their creative potential.

Emotional Support

If children are to think in creative ways, they need a teacher and classroom environment that are respectful of their responses, suggestions, and ideas. An emotionally safe environment allows children to attempt different things without fear of criticism or derision from their teacher or peers, which enables their ideas to bloom or, if a child so chooses, be forgotten. They understand that a masterpiece or perfection is not expected each time they try something new, and that even when they fail, they can still learn from an unsuccessful endeavor. Because they feel supported in their efforts, they are comfortable venturing into new territory, making mistakes, and trying again (and again!).

You establish a supportive environment by building positive relationships with each child and accepting their uniqueness, mistakes, capabilities, and challenges. Help children learn how to collaborate with others, value their ideas, and mentor those who need support. Mentors and partners—such as a child who understands the solution to a problem assisting an inexperienced child who faces that same problem—can work together to grow in their confidence and abilities. In this respectful environment, all children feel accepted.

Ana and Ben's Story

Ana (age 4), whose parents are from China, attends a child care center in the United States. She speaks fluent Chinese and English and is very proud of her language abilities. She says to her teacher, "You know, Ms. Sarah, I am taking French class now." Ms. Sarah responds, "Wow, Ana, that is impressive! How many languages do you speak?" Ana eloquently replies, "I speak three now. And I am also learning how to swim at the swimming pool near my house."

Ben (age 4) says, "I hate water. I don't like swimming." Ms. Sarah responds to both children. "Ana, I see you are learning a new language and swimming during the week. Ben, I understand that you don't like water; I also did not like water when I was little." Ben smiles and Ana responds, "Ben, I can teach you how to swim!" His face lights up. "I want to learn how to jump in the water!" "Okay!" Ana agrees.

Story Reflection

Ana, who participates in many afterschool activities, enjoys talking about her weekly schedule with her friends. Ben, on the other hand, loves to play with his younger brother at home. Sometimes children like Ben may be sensitive to experiences their classmates have that are different from their own. Notice that Sarah responds by simply repeating what each child has mentioned. To help Ben feel included, she adds her support by sharing her personal feelings about water. Knowing Ana's propensity to share her interests with others, Ms. Sarah helps her understand Ben's perspective. As a result, Ana quickly offers to teach Ben how to swim. This further makes Ben feel included and accepted. Modeling acceptance of differences and finding a way for children to collaborate helps create a safe, nurturing environment for everyone.

Jill is listening to Carmelia (age 4) describe the festival that will take place in her community over the weekend. Jill is learning about Carmelia's culture, celebrations, and family participation, which will help Jill plan activities and materials that will be supportive of Carmelia and engage the other children as well.

Reigniting the Fire: Nurture Your Own Creativity

Most early childhood teachers are creative, although some may not recognize that they are. Sometimes teachers are forced to meet the expectations of others, which may curb their creative expression and their desire to pursue new ways of doing things. Teachers who feel that they are not creative can recapture their creative spirit as they work with young children and observe their remarkable play and delightful ideas. Watching and enjoying the ways young children think, play, and solve problems can inspire teachers to consider possibilities and experiment with new approaches themselves.

Here are some suggestions for nurturing your own creativity and making time for creative pursuits.

Be childlike. In our busy lives, it can be easy to overlook or stop appreciating the beauty in our world. Find happiness around you by enjoying both the small and the more significant things. Take time to examine new ideas and materials and reexamine old ones. By taking pleasure in the beauty around you, you can recapture a sense of wonder and better understand how children feel each day.

Be open to new experiences. Trying something new challenges you to think and explore in innovative ways. Commute to school or work using a different route or mode of transportation—instead of driving, take advantage of the first warm day of the season to ride your bike to work. Wear a hat or other item of clothing that you've never worn before. Try a new recipe with different ingredients, or create a dish using what you have on hand. Take a class. Seek out a different genre of book or music than what you typically read or listen to, or sing the children a song you haven't shared with them.

Foster a playful attitude. Experience the intrinsic joy of playing—with different materials, stories, and words. Relearn the power of playfulness, the motivation it inspires, and the enjoyment you receive from it.

Read about creative people, their work, and the things that inspire them. Many artists and creative thinkers remember powerful experiences from their childhood, special places where they could imagine and create, and people who supported their ideas, art, experimentation, or music. They talk about the freedom they felt in play and a significant person who recognized their creative ability. Their stories indicate how important early support is for the developing thinker, artist, scientist, or musician. Find something that inspires you—a photograph, quote, story, or piece of music—and let it help you create or think in new ways.

Grow professionally. Read professional books or journals, attend conferences, collaborate with colleagues, and visit other classrooms and programs to learn the latest information and spark new ideas. These experiences can help you expand your thinking and consider new approaches to teaching.

Reflections

› How do particular children in your classroom exhibit characteristics of a creative person?

› What special interests do the children in your classroom have? What opportunities and choices can you provide so children can follow their individual interests?

› Have you recently tried something new? Reflect on the event. How did you feel during the experience? What other possibilities might you pursue? If you haven't taken a first step toward new experiences, think about what you could try.

› Do you engage in open-ended activities that allow you to be creative, make choices, and follow your passions? What are they, and how have you grown from these experiences?

› Have you observed children of diverse abilities involved in creative activities? Describe some of the situations where children demonstrated their creativity.

The teacher has set up a story table that includes a felt cloth, miniature animals, rocks, bricks, dolls, and bones.

A small group of children come t[o] the story table and begin explori[ng] the items.

Emma (age 3) is telling [the] teacher her story abou[t] the animals looking for the bones that she an[d] her friend have hidden [in] the mountain.

These two children experiment with ways to hide the bones inside the felt mountain.

After finding the bones, Cliff (age 3) says, "The dogs and cats are thirsty and they need water. The end."

Chapter 5

What Is the Teacher's Role?

The most powerful way to develop creativity in your students is to be a role model. Children develop creativity not when you tell them to, but when you show them.

—Robert Sternberg and Wendy M. Williams, "Teaching for Creativity: Two Dozen Tips," Center for Development and Learning (blog)

eachers who are dedicated to nurturing the *whole child* recognize that this includes creativity and the arts. Understanding that creativity happens everywhere and often in unexpected ways is critical to providing a supportive environment infused with opportunities for creative expression. This chapter discusses specific strategies for encouraging the development of children's creative thinking.

Supporting the Development of Creativity

You are responsible for planning and implementing a program that supports young children's learning and development in many domains. You ultimately decide what to teach, but these choices are affected by your school or program, the community, families, government agencies, and professional organizations. There is a lot to juggle; for example, you have the difficult yet exciting task of providing appropriate experiences to foster digital literacy, a skill that will be crucial to children's success in school and beyond. Three-year-old Hayley tries to swipe the pages of a print book from left to right because she is used to reading books on a tablet and sliding her finger across the screen. What would you do in this situation? Encourage Hayley's parents to provide only print books for her to read, or embrace a variety of avenues for reading and learning? You have the opportunity to inspire creative children by providing a diverse array of meaningful and developmentally appropriate classroom experiences that nurture thinking and hone their skills.

Valuing Creative Thinking

The first step in this complex process is recognizing that creativity, collaboration, communication, and critical thinking are essential elements in a program designed to inspire the development of imagination and problem-solving skills. As an observant and knowledgeable teacher, you recognize children's creative thinking, appreciate its importance, and encourage children to try new things and take some appropriate risks. Young children are the epitome of creative thinkers, and recognizing their abilities and valuing the development of imagination make your classroom a place where thinking and innovative ideas grow. A teacher who believes in the importance of creative thinking communicates her support of children's ideas, provides materials that challenge their thinking, and displays their work in the classroom.

Partnering With Children

Historically, teachers have been dispensers of knowledge. They determined what should be learned and then imparted this information to the children for them to absorb, memorize, and reproduce the "correct" answers. However, for children to succeed in today's world and that of the future, they must be active participants in the learning process—asking questions, observing, thinking about ideas, and exploring topics and ideas deeply. In a classroom designed to inspire creative thinking and problem solving, the teacher is a co-learner with the children. In Reggio Emilia–inspired programs and other settings that value initiative taking, teachers observe, listen, scaffold, and offer support as the children make discoveries, attempt to clarify their own thinking, and determine the direction of their work. In these programs, the teacher is both an observer and a learner who provides a model for children as they try to find answers to their questions. The children's ideas are valued, teachers learn from their comments, and the work is enriched by ideas and suggestions from both the teacher and the children. This interactive process enables teachers to have meaningful conversations with children and nurture their creative thinking (Edwards, Gandini, & Forman 1998).

Creative Teachers and Creative Teaching

A teacher who is creative and brings out creativity in children recognizes the importance of creative thinking and uses it in her own actions, which positively impacts the development of creativity in young children. Several studies have identified some characteristics that correlate with nurturing creativity in children. In an early study, Torrance (1962) found that children in kindergarten and the primary grades made the most significant gains in creativity when they worked with teachers who were interested in the creative processes. In another study, Thompson, Greer, and Greer (2004) asked university students to recall the characteristics of one of their most creative and influential teachers. Some students remembered their teacher giving them recognition when they were younger and how that experience helped them gain confidence.

Creative teachers and creative teaching are key components in fostering young children's creativity. Many have described the teacher's role in balancing structure and freedom of expression. Carol Sharp (2004) and Carolyn Edwards and Kay Springate (1995) identify several ways teachers nurture creative thinking, including

> Asking open-ended questions
> Offering choices
> Modeling creative thinking and behaviors
> Encouraging experimentation and persistence
> Recognizing individual ways of learning
> Allowing children to pursue their interests
> Enabling children to work independently or in small groups
> Supporting children while they work at their own pace and in their own way

Esquivel (1995) suggests that teachers who enhance children's creativity are often flexible, open-minded, have a sense of humor, and can be spontaneous in their classrooms. Renzulli and De Wet (2010) state that the "ultimate goal for learning is to replace dependency and passive learning with independence and engaged learning" (38). They propose that the teacher's challenge is to become a facilitator of learning rather than the disseminator of information. The creative teacher's role is to assist in problem solving and to help children understand how to use resources and materials to engage in deep learning.

Providing Support and Experiences Throughout the Day

Look for ways to infuse your program with opportunities for children to predict and test what will happen as they work with materials or participate in activities across domains. For example, several children might remark that when they rinse their brushes in glasses of water, the tempera paint swirls around and gradually disperses into the water. You could ask what would happen if they dripped oil paint into a plastic tub with an inch of water. Ask for predictions, see what happens, compare the result to the predictions, and ask children for their ideas on what happened and why. "The King's Drum," a retelling of an Anansi African folktale in *Tell It Again! Easy-to-Tell Stories With Activities for Young Children* (1999), by Shirley C. Raines and Rebecca Isbell, can be used to investigate communicating with drums. After reading the story, introduce children to a basic drumbeat and invite them to echo the rhythm. Then ask them to create new, individual patterns to respond to each other's drumbeats. Ask questions to extend their thinking: "How would you send a quick message on the drum to your friends?," "What if they were far away?," and "How could you send a secret message to a friend?"

Meaningful experiences and everyday routines can help develop creative thinking when you give children time to influence the process and solve their own problems. During snack time, a child is challenged to determine if there are enough apple slices for every child in the class. What are some of the possible ways the child can solve the problem? Does he count the children in the class or the number of apple slices? Perhaps he estimates based on the size of the container he is holding. How would you facilitate the child's thinking? As an integral part of the creative thinking process, you observe, use active listening, question, document, reflect, and determine other resources you might use to extend thinking. A creative teacher is not just a supporter—he is an active inspirer who brings in his own resources and experiences to share with children and stimulate new ideas. He also senses when to let children take ownership of their ideas and follow their agendas.

Susanna's Story

When composing a story about Chocolate Chip, the class guinea pig, a small group of preschool children contributes several words and phrases to describe their pet. Susanna, their teacher, asks questions to draw out their ideas and language to create a group story (literacy).

In the dramatic play center, two children discuss how to arrange the recycled grocery items that have been donated to their classroom. They discuss whether to put the large items together or the red containers together. One suggests that they should read the labels to decide how to arrange them. Together they identify many possible ways to store the items—by size, color, and function (math). Ultimately, they decide to arrange the recycled items by size.

When involved in an art project, Marcos (age 5) experiments with potter's clay for the first time. He is intrigued by how it feels and the way it responds differently from the playdough he often uses. "It's cold and hard, but I like it because the shape stays when I want to place something on top!" Marcos exclaims. He pats the clay flat, punches holes with his fingers, and pushes shells into the clay (art).

During cleanup time, Susanna challenges the children to move like an animal of their choosing as they put the toys and materials away.

Reflection

These observations of children's thinking show that creativity occurs across the curriculum, during routines, and throughout the day. You can also see how the teacher thoughtfully and deliberately supports children's creative thinking by encouraging observations and descriptions (creating a story about the guinea pig), introducing a problem to solve (how to organize and store the food items), and offering extensions and providing intriguing materials the children can experiment with and combine in new ways (putting out shells near the potter's clay).

Providing Choices and Options

Children need choices that allow them to direct and control their experiences. Gaining experience in making decisions sets children on a path to being self-directed learners who can think for themselves, evaluate possibilities more deliberately, and take responsibility for the outcomes. When children are able to influence their world through personal choices, they gain confidence in their ability to make decisions and take ownership of their learning, which makes it more salient. Some of these are limited choices, such as which center a child wants to work in on a particular day. Other situations will offer a broader range of options; to showcase what they learned during a project, a group of children might consider whether to produce a mural, photographs, a book, a drama, a musical rendition, or a combination of options.

For children who have limited experience in decision making, it is helpful to start by offering fewer possibilities for them to consider. As they become more comfortable with making choices, provide more options. Children may also change their minds and decide to try a different choice. Trial and error and discovering what works for them is part of the learning process.

Look for ways to incorporate child choice even into teacher-initiated activities. And when you do so, be flexible and willing to accept children's decisions. This means giving up some control of what is happening and supporting children in what they have decided.

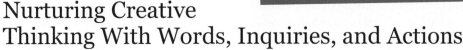

"Which painting tool would you like to choose?"

Nurturing Creative Thinking With Words, Inquiries, and Actions

There are many ways to encourage children's ideas, responses, work, and creative thinking. Smiling at a child who is making up a new dance with a friend communicates that you recognize and enjoy his inventiveness. Saying a few descriptive words about a child's project indicates your interest and may provide the child with a new idea. Moving closer to a child who is focused on building a miniature structure with paper clips and paper indicates your curiosity about the complexity of the design. Inviting another child to observe a classmate's project can encourage collaboration. Asking questions and making encouraging suggestions can help children move forward with their ideas when they become frustrated. A teacher who understands the creative process, including the incubation period, may ask questions like "Would you like to put this on the shelf and return to it tomorrow?" or "What do you think you'll need for the next step?"

Tsitsi's Class's Story

A group of preschool children take a field trip to the local grocery store. Before the trip, they discussed where they were going, generated ideas about what they might see, and discussed some of their questions. At the grocery store, they explore the produce department, the meat section, and other areas that are interesting to them. They also talk to the manager, cashiers, and stock people. At the end of the excursion, each child purchases a vegetable, all of which are used to make vegetable soup when they return to the classroom.

As an additional follow-up activity, Tsitsi, their teacher, asks children to draw a picture of something they saw or a person they talked to at the grocery store. However, none of the children's pictures is about the grocery store or the people who work there. She wonders what the children learned from the visit. Several days later, however, a few of the children begin to draw pictures of colorful fruit and

vegetable displays, shelves of cereal, and items set up around the checkout registers.

Reflection

This is a well-planned field trip that includes preparation beforehand. The children see many things during the visit. At the grocery store and while they are on the bus to and from the store, Tsitsi talks to the children, listens to their questions, and discusses their experiences. The children enjoy selecting the vegetables they purchase for the soup they make. So why don't the children draw pictures about their trip on the day of the visit? Perhaps they need time to think about all the things they experience and for their thoughts and drawings to incubate. This concept is supported by the observation that several days later, some of the children in the art area begin to draw and paint what they saw at the store.

Seeing the Importance of Risk and Mistakes

Whenever a teacher or child tries a new idea or does something differently, he takes a risk: each attempt has the potential to fail. An old adage says, "Anyone who has never made a mistake has never tried anything new." Taking a risk, guessing, or trying something different can be difficult. Most people, including children, are more hesitant to take risks in an environment where conformity is expected and rewarded. Taking a leap into the unknown is scary, and many adults and children do not enjoy taking risks because of past failures or negative experiences.

However, the majority of innovations, experiments, inventions, writings, and designs happen because the creator deviates from convention. In a classroom that inspires creative thinking, teachers and children learn to be comfortable taking risks and making mistakes, both of which are an important part of learning, discovering new ideas, and refining the process of creating.

One way to encourage children to branch out and try new things is to ask open-ended questions and provide supportive, nonjudgmental comments that keep children's ideas flowing, such as the examples featured in Figure 5.1 on page 85. Remember to consider your facial expressions, gestures, intonation, and wait time. When posing any questions or providing support, listen carefully and reflect on what a child is sharing. Some teachers, while well intentioned, ask a barrage of open-ended questions while children are involved in something, which can easily frustrate children or cause them to lose interest in their own ideas. Make sure the questions you ask are genuine, judicious, and help children think more deeply about what they are doing and what they want to achieve. Then give them time to consider and respond to your questions at their own pace. Listening to children is a critical part of providing appropriate words, questions, and support.

Accidental Inventions

The ideas and experiments of inventors, scientists, and artists have led to many great inventions and innovations. Other products or techniques were discovered by accident or resulted from a mistake. Take, for example, the 3M Post-it Note. In 1968, Spencer Silver was trying to invent a strong adhesive while working in the 3M laboratory (Hiskey 2011; NCFL 2015). He was successful in developing a new type of glue, but it was actually very weak. He was disappointed with the results because it did not stick in the way he had planned, so he moved on to other experiments. Five years later, another scientist from 3M, Art Fry, was singing in his church choir and wanted to mark the pages in his hymnal, but his paper markers kept falling out. He remembered his colleague's invention, decided to coat paper scraps with the weak glue, and voila! Today, self-adhesive notes are one of the most popular office products in the world (NCFL 2015).

If young children feel that adults support and treasure their novel ideas, they are more willing to try out new possibilities. They know that their experimentation will be accepted and supported. Help children understand that mistakes are part of the creative process. Share moments or stories that demonstrate mistakes you have made and how you learned from them. This sharing can reassure children that it is okay to make mistakes and not be perfect, and that our mistakes can teach us valuable lessons.

A less confident child may watch and observe what happens when other children contribute an unusual idea. In a supportive environment, she sees that you relish children's suggestions

Figure 5.1 Keep the Creativity Flowing: Questions and Phrases That Support Creative Thinking

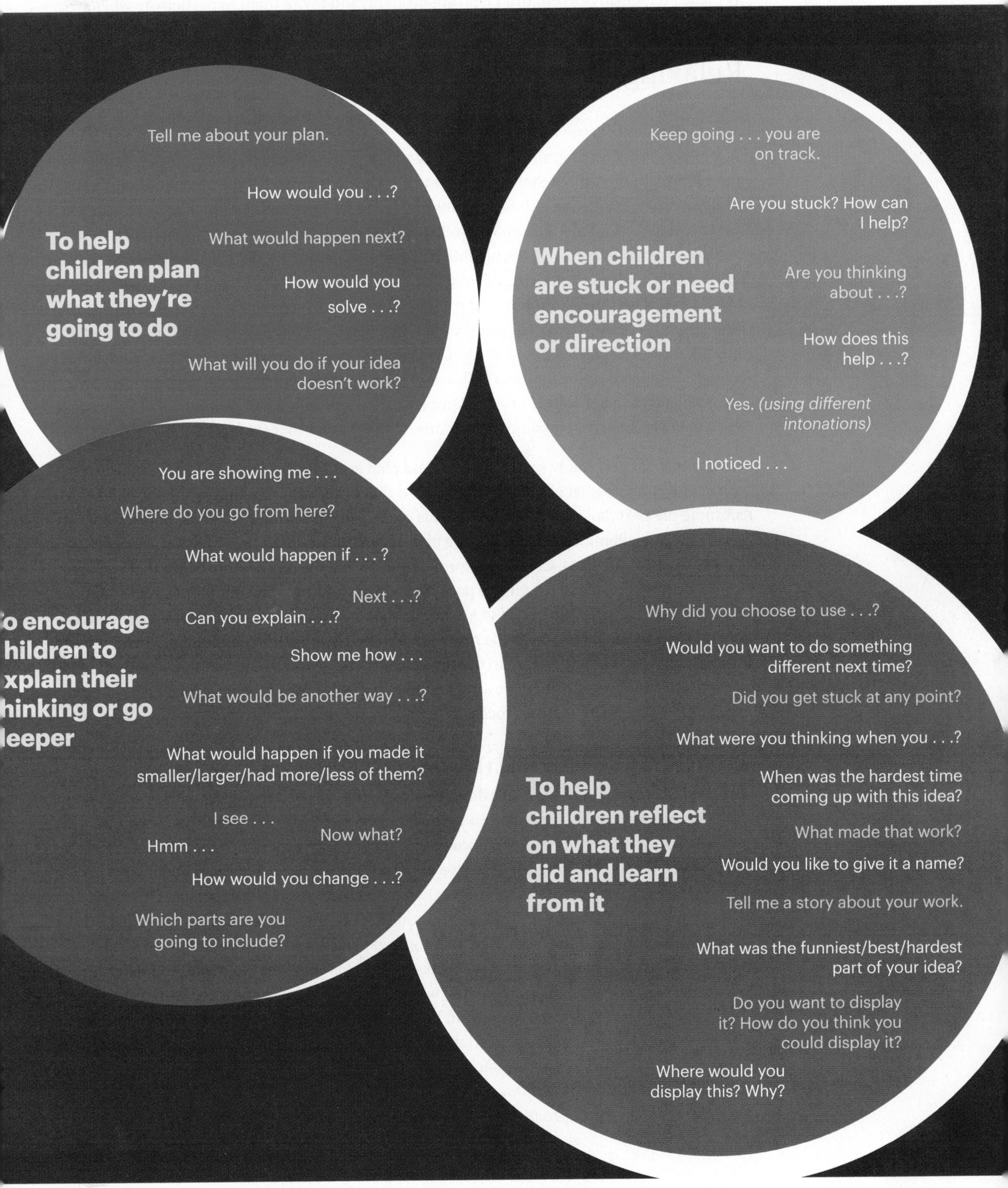

To help children plan what they're going to do

Tell me about your plan.

How would you . . .?

What would happen next?

How would you solve . . .?

What will you do if your idea doesn't work?

When children are stuck or need encouragement or direction

Keep going . . . you are on track.

Are you stuck? How can I help?

Are you thinking about . . .?

How does this help . . .?

Yes. *(using different intonations)*

I noticed . . .

To encourage children to explain their thinking or go deeper

You are showing me . . .

Where do you go from here?

What would happen if . . . ?

Next . . .?

Can you explain . . .?

Show me how . . .

What would be another way . . .?

What would happen if you made it smaller/larger/had more/less of them?

I see . . .

Hmm . . .

Now what?

How would you change . . .?

Which parts are you going to include?

To help children reflect on what they did and learn from it

Why did you choose to use . . .?

Would you want to do something different next time?

Did you get stuck at any point?

What were you thinking when you . . .?

When was the hardest time coming up with this idea?

What made that work?

Would you like to give it a name?

Tell me a story about your work.

What was the funniest/best/hardest part of your idea?

Do you want to display it? How do you think you could display it?

Where would you display this? Why?

or inquire about their ideas. Later, this child might feel more confident and willing to try something new, make suggestions, and be less concerned about the possibility of negative feedback. Be sensitive to children who are hesitant, and invite them to participate whenever they wish and when an opportunity arises.

Relaxing Time Constraints

Creative thinking, complex projects, and collaboration take time. Have you ever been told you have 15 minutes to come up with a new idea for an existing problem? In this situation, it is not uncommon to become paralyzed and unable to come up with even one idea, much less several alternatives. In the United States and many other societies, there is a tremendous emphasis on time—when things begin, how long they last, and when to end. Reggio Emilia teachers in Italy provide a useful model, one with relaxed time constraints and an approach that allows children and teachers to dive deeply into a project, experiment with different approaches, and reflect on discoveries. Removing all your time restraints may not be possible or practical, but you can begin to think about relaxing some limitations. On some occasions, try following the interests of the children, allowing additional time when a project is really rolling and ideas are spiking. When you begin to have more flexibility in your schedule and extend time for children's interests and ideas, you will be surprised at the results—detailed work, expanded projects, and stronger collaboration. Complex ideas and projects are more likely to emerge when children have time to more fully immerse themselves in learning.

To help this happen, know each child well and plan accordingly. For a child who may need more time, prepare a set of strategies to extend that time, either by suggesting the child continue the next day or taking photographs of the project so that the child can re-create it another time. Remind the child during play or other times of the day that she can work on her project if she likes. Creating a special time during the day demonstrates that you are supportive and flexible to the child's pace. Sometimes adding a few minutes to center time or project work allows children who are immersed in a project to complete or add to their work. When you cannot expand the time, explain the reason to the children and involve them in coming up with ways to adapt to the time constraints. These are initial steps for finding ways to keep the creative juices flowing and to eliminate some of the time barriers that often interrupt or stall the inventive process.

Extending, Revisiting, and Reflecting

Another aspect related to time and flow is encouraging children to persist with an idea or project over an extended time. Your schedule may be filled with activities that begin and end in one day, making it hard or impossible for children to experience the positive effects of sustained work (revisiting what they've done, adding features, and including more depth to the implementation of their ideas) on projects. When children are able to return to and continue with their work, the details and expressions are significantly extended. An opportunity to, for example, edit their writing or expand a science experiment over time allows children to evaluate their work, think of additions they want to make, and determine what is needed to support or improve the work. If a child has an unfinished story he is dictating, find extra time to continue and help him find a place to keep it until then. During the day or during transition time, initiate a conversation by inquiring how the child would like to end his story. Small reminders such as this may trigger the child's thinking and assist him in revisiting and evaluating his work. Take time to reflect with children and demonstrate how thinking about a project can result in inventive extensions.

Supporting children's ability to evaluate their own efforts and come up ways they can improve or do something differently will help them become less dependent on the approval of others. To this end, be careful about evaluating a child's creative work or using comments that carry judgment, even positive judgment, such as "That's good" or "Beautiful!" It is often more beneficial to encourage children to look critically at their own efforts by asking them questions such as "Which one of your stories should I post on the school blog?," "What do you like about this story?," and "Why do you like it more than that one?" Help children look at their work from different perspectives: "What part of this collage you made for your sister do you think she will like the most?," "Where do you think your sculpture would get more light?," and "Do you think Kalim would like to display his creation on this table too?" Learning to evaluate one's own work is a difficult task and takes years and much experience to refine. Being able to critique and self-evaluate is a skill needed by writers, musicians, artists, mathematicians, chefs, engineers, dancers, technology experts—just about everyone.

When you do comment on a child's work, use specific statements that relate to what you observe the child focusing on. If a child is dipping one finger into paint and carefully placing that finger on a piece of paper, looking at her finger, and then repeating the process with her other fingers, what might you say to support this experimentation? A comment like "I see you're using purple and yellow," while nonjudgmental, is not reflective of what seems important to her at that moment. Asked at an appropriate moment—such as when the child turns to you and shows you her fingers—a comment such as "Oh, you have a dab of paint on each finger, and I can see where you pressed the paint hard on your paper. I wonder what you will do next with the paint" connects the two of you to the child's activity and invites her to extend her experiment.

When to Join, When to Provide Support, and When to Step Back

Determining when to involve yourself during a child's creative process and how frequently can be challenging. Each situation is different, each group of children is diverse, and each child's needs, abilities, skills, and temperament vary. Knowing each child and carefully observing the situation will help you determine when to intervene, suggest another child help or be consulted, offer a suggestion, or let the child struggle a bit and work it out alone. In some instances you might move in too quickly, which does not allow children to determine how to wrestle with an issue or project. Observe, think, and ask yourself, "Can she figure this out on her own?," "Where is this going?," and "Is he getting too frustrated?" If a child demolishes his block structure because it is wobbling, wait to see what the child does next. Does he rebuild using a new strategy? Or is he too upset to try a different approach? Sometimes, listening and adding encouraging comments will be sufficient. Other times, a child will need your direct intervention or suggestions. It is not always easy to decide, which is one reason why teaching is often referred to as an art.

The teacher asks the child (age 4) questions about the color and design she wants to use on her t-shirt.

Mindmapping: A Practical Tool for Teachers to Generate and Organize Creative Ideas

When you are searching for innovative ideas, unique solutions, and ways to motivate yourself to use divergent thinking, *mindmaps* are one way to gain clarity and explore the issue. This is an active approach to encourage divergent, unconventional thinking that helps you generate more ideas. Mindmapping helps organize your thoughts visually; Figure 5.2 shows an example based on the central theme of "Nurturing My Creativity." Some people find that visually mapping and webbing can help them identify ideas, extensions, and expansions. This versatile technique can be used in a variety of situations, ranging from planning low-cost dinners (a personal issue) to finding free materials for the invention center in your classroom (a professional issue). The map helps you access ideas from a central focus (the defined problem). The further you expand from the central idea, the more ideas you will uncover. As you branch out from the center, ask yourself, "What else can I add that relates to this theme?" Some of your ideas will lead to another whole cluster of possibilities. Keep adding options until your ideas slow. As you persist, your mind will open up to ideas just waiting to become part of the mindmap. Once you feel your mindmap is comprehensive, ask, "How can I use these ideas?" Sometimes a to-do list encouraged by mindmapping will lead to action and a solution that you might not have identified when you began the process.

Figure 5.2 Mindmap

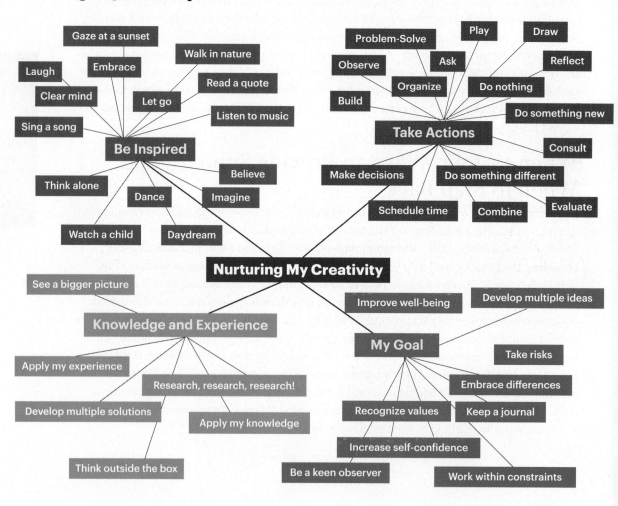

Nurturing Creativity: An Essential Mindset for Young Children's Learning

Mindmapping can also be used with children as a tool to record and extend their ideas during group meeting or project time. For example, at the end of the year one of the teachers in a program will retire. Another teacher asks the children, "What can we make as a gift for Miss Ella?" The children suggest taking a group picture, making a book that includes their drawings, putting together a quilt, and decorating a clay container to hold flowers. These elements can be included in a mindmap, providing a visual representation of their ideas and suggestions.

You have a tremendous impact on the attitudes, learning, language, and creative thinking of the children you teach. You embody a model the children can emulate, a thinker they can admire, and a designer who develops a supportive environment where their creative ideas can take root and bloom.

Early childhood education teachers attending the NAEYC Professional Learning Institute.

Reflections

› A child shows you a sculpture he composed of feathers, clay, and colored wire. What would be your first thought? What would you say or do? How might you respond to help the child evaluate his own efforts?

› What new children's book would you like to read to children? How might you prepare for the sharing? Think about questions you could ask the children about the story before and after you read it together. How can you extend the story in a unique way?

› Challenge yourself to think of several possibilities for an experience, project, or activity and determine which of your ideas will allow you and/or the children to try new things.

Renee recognizes her pre-K class's interest in dinosaurs and provides clay to extend their creative thinking.

Renee asks the chil[...] an open-ended qu[...] "How can you use [...] with a dinosaur?"

Margaret (age 3) decides to make meat and grass for her dinosaur to eat.

Malik (age 3) determines that his dinosaur needs a big, thick cape.

Emmett (age 4) makes shoes and a mask. He takes models of the foot and face to make sure the items fit.

"The dinosaur is very hungry . . . so I made a special power orange grass to eat!" Emmett exclaims. "And then, he can fly!"

Chapter 6

The Role of Play in Creativity

As in all development and learning in the early years, play is the medium for learning, and the foundation for creative development.

—Doireann O'Connor, *Educational Tales of the Unexpected: Children and Creativity*

Play is essential in the lives of all children. When children play, they build on what they already know by using their imaginations to create and work through pretend scenarios. Play gives children a safe way to learn, try out ideas, interact with peers, and make sense of their world without consequences through exploring, pretending, and testing (Brown & Vaughan 2010).

Many theorists, researchers, and experts have written about the positive influence of play on children's development. Piaget (1954) explains that thinking and playing are interconnected, with each affecting the other. Vygotsky ([1930–35] 1978) explains that during play, children use language to accompany their activity and move to higher levels of understanding. Fröebel's ([1826] 2005) early kindergarten was built around children using *gifts* (educational materials) that they manipulated, experimented with, and learned from. Gardner (2011) extends our understanding of play to include children using thinking, language, movement, and the arts in meaningful activity. Zigler and Valentine (1979) state that play provides the opportunity for children to talk, collaborate, and problem-solve. Wendy Smolen (2015), co-founder of Sandbox Summit, which conducts the annual Sandbox Summit@MIT on creative play, writes that open-ended play stimulates creativity and fosters the critical thinking skills needed for the twenty-first century. Playful environments support creative thinking as young children shape their play by choosing materials, communicating with others, participating in continual problem solving, and collaborating on what to do, when to do it, and how.

Why Is Play Important to Creativity?

When children play, they are

> Intensely involved

> Internally motivated

> Enjoying the process

> Persistent

> Imaginative

> Taking different perspectives and risks

Because play is a transformational activity, it allows children to participate in their own way and be successful in the process. Children of varying capabilities and personal experiences are able to play and work together. Play is important for helping children reach important social, emotional, and cognitive developmental milestones (Milteer & Ginsburg 2012). It helps children cope with problems and adjust to changes. An important skill for creative thinking is the ability to identify problems and adapt thinking to new issues; in play, children build these skills in an environment where risks and mistakes are valued as part of the experimentation process.

To design an effective play environment that supports creativity (Broadhead 2004), consider these three steps:

1. **Carefully select materials** that require the greatest input from a child. For instance, adding a large sponge to the water table will inspire a child to explore the properties of the sponge, determine how much water it can absorb, and find many different ways to extract water from it. He might scrub with it, stack several sponges, stuff a sponge into a funnel to block the flow of water, or use it for countless other purposes.

2. **Be attentive.** Observe where children are in their development and what catches their attention. Consider how you can use their interests to weave in opportunities for creative play and learning, and watch for children to use materials in surprising ways. Soraya, a lead preschool teacher, set up a "shoe store" in her classroom after noting the children's interest in a shoe store during their field trip to a mall. She included several types of shoes and empty shoeboxes to encourage the children to sort the shoes and place them in the boxes. Some of the children thought of an alternative use for the shoeboxes and began to stack and arrange them in a tall, abstract design. They then selected a pair of red, sparkly shoes and displayed them on top of their shoebox structure with a price tag that said $25. After observing their play, Soraya said, "You came up with a unique design to display those glittery shoes!"

3. **Respect children's choices and believe in their wisdom** about their learning needs. With the classroom's shoe store, Soraya respected the children's choices and recognized that their way of using the shoeboxes was more interesting than what she had envisioned—sorting pairs of shoes into boxes. Soraya valued the children's innovation and understood their desire for playing in a different way.

Types of Play and the Development of Creativity

During the early years, there are many different types of play that enhance children's creative development. Below we'll explore a few kinds in more detail: sensory and exploratory play, symbolic play, construction play, and pretend and socio-dramatic play. Creative dramatics, storytelling, and musical improvisation and composition are also important play activities for stimulating creativity. Children may move in and out of these different types of play over time and in varied settings.

Sensory and Exploratory Play

During sensory and exploratory play (play with objects), children examine the qualities of materials and items in their world. This exploration supports their curiosity as they investigate different ways to learn about objects, such as comparing or contrasting and finding identifying features. Children also use their senses to extend their understanding of objects and explore the effects of movement and repeating actions: What is this? What does it feel like? What sounds does it make? Can I taste it? What does it smell like? What can I do with it? What other things can I use with it?

To support this type of play, provide open-ended materials that offer rich exploration for children's senses, including various types of sand and mud; water and ice cubes; twigs; rocks of various colors, textures, and shapes; and fabrics, such as leather, fake fur, plastic, burlap, and silk. Children approach and respond to sensory learning in different ways. One child may be hesitant to touch or manipulate clay, while another might be fascinated by the feel of

Erik (age 3) is surprised by the feel of the foam. He is not sure he likes it.

potter's clay and will spend a long time experimenting with it (Isbell & Isbell 2008). Let children explore new items in their own way and at their own pace. If children are hesitant, look for ways they can have a similar sensory experience, such as squishing paint sealed in a plastic bag.

The first step in learning about and using something new is to explore its properties. For instance, the first time Jonathan discovers a piece of crinkled foil in the recycling bin, he explores it in several ways. First, he mashes the foil flat, trying to get all the wrinkles out. Next, he rolls the foil into a ball and then squashes the shape into different forms. Then, he tears small pieces from the foil, experimenting with each piece to see what happens when he flattens, squashes, and tears it. After extensive experimentation and examination, Jonathan uses the foil to cover a side of his fire truck.

Pellegrini and Gustafson (2005) observed 3- to 5-year-olds over the course of a school year. They found that the amount of playful exploration children engaged in predicted their performance on physical problem-solving tasks. Playing with objects and tools that invite children to make, change, or build things (such as wood pieces, rocks of various textures and shapes, and construction paper) ignites children's curiosity and allows them to explore, set goals, challenge their own thinking, and improve their problem-finding and problem-solving strategies.

Sergio's Story

Four-year-old Sergio is from Brazil and has never seen snow. After a class discussion about the children's experience with snow, Mariko, his preschool teacher, uses ice cubes to make lots of shaved ice with the children. They put the shaved ice in the middle of the empty water table. Small groups of children explore the snow-like properties of the shaved ice, scoop it with small shovels, and mold it into shapes. Some children even taste it. Sergio is hesitant to touch the ice at first, but when he sees his friends playing, he joins in. He pokes the soft flakes of ice, squishes some with his fingers, and is surprised to see that it melts in front of his eyes. Then he scoops a big bunch with both hands and fashions it into a small sphere. "Snowman?" Sergio asks Mariko, and she nods. "Snow-cold-MAN!" Sergio

shouts with joy. Soon all the shaved ice melts into water, but Mariko makes sure to capture Sergio's reaction with the mobile camera she always carries in her pocket.

Reflection

A new experience can be scary but also exciting. Being sensitive to children's backgrounds and encouraging them to explore materials and properties in their own ways opens the door to creative ideas, like Sergio's one-sphered snowman. Being gradually exposed to a novel material gives Sergio the confidence to investigate it and use it to create something, moving beyond the exploratory stage and surprising his teacher with his creative idea.

Before putting the rubber chips on the playground into a cup, this child experienced their squishyness under her feet and in her hands.

Symbolic Play

During the preschool years, children grow in their ability to use symbols in their play. Throughout their lives, children will use many symbolic systems, including spoken language, reading, writing, numbers, music, and various visual media, including painting and drawing. Initially children use realistic symbols, such as a wooden block to represent a car or a piece of cord for a snake. Each item has some resemblance to the object being represented. As their ability to use symbolic representations expands, children use more abstract symbols that look less like the actual object as they create stories and art, perform scientific experiments, or collaborate on group projects. Several blocks might represent a skyscraper; scribbles on paper stand for a "No food or drink" sign on the door of a child-designed "medical center." With a teacher's assistance, one child covers a suspended Hula-Hoop with sheer, soft fabric and names it "Space Time Machine."

Vladimir and Louis's Story

The science center in Ms. Tonya's pre-K classroom contains many interesting items for children to examine, explore, and manipulate. For several weeks, many children have visited this area and investigated several types, shapes, and sizes of leaves. Noticing that fewer children are choosing to go to the area, Ms. Tonya adds a novel item for the children to investigate: a flexible, expandable silver tube (used as a vent for a clothes dryer and purchased at a home repair store). Vladimir and Louis (both 4 years old) are curious about this object. They begin by feeling it and repeatedly expanding and compacting the tube. They talk to figure out what's going on: "What is this?," "Is there a wire inside?," and "How long can we stretch it?" They bend the tube into a circle, roll it around on the floor, and go back to stretching it. Over an extended period of time, they thoroughly investigate this strange item. They decide to take turns pretending to be elephants, using the tube as their trunk.

Reflection

Feeling that adding the expandable dryer vent to the science center will provide a new spark for the children's investigation, Ms. Tonya is interested to see what happens. She observes as two children explore the properties and possible uses of the silver tube. At times, she poses questions to expand their thinking and scaffolds their ideas. She is so intrigued by their curiosity and the varied ways they examine the new material that she decides to take photographs and document their exploration of the item. Her addition of a novel item to the science area and her documentation of the boys' investigation provide evidence of their play and creative thinking.

These girls are caring for a baby doll on the playground. Together they are giving the baby milk from a large container.

Jasmin and Kesha's Story

Jasmin and Kesha (both age 4) are in a Head Start program. Their teacher has set up a well-designed dramatic play center that includes a bedroom and two child-size rocking chairs. Each girl selects a doll, which they talk to, rock, and comfort by singing. Jasmin notices a collection of books in a basket next to the rocking chairs. She selects one of her favorite books, which the teacher has read during circle time, and returns to the rocking chairs holding her baby in her arms. Together, Jasmin and Kesha begin to read the story in their own words to their baby dolls, turning each page and holding the book so that the babies can see.

Reflection

Jasmin and Kesha are involved in symbolic play as they use baby dolls to represent real babies. They emulate ways they have seen adults interact with babies, including talking in high-pitched voices, sitting in rocking chairs, and comforting them. The teacher has carefully set up the area to include dolls of diverse ethnicity, child-size rocking chairs, and a collection of books the children are familiar with. This environment encourages children's symbolic play and extends their actions to include reading to their babies.

Construction Play

During construction play, children build, combine materials, or produce intricate structures. This play is observed in the block area, the invention center, and the art studio, and during indoor or outdoor play with loose parts. Children extend their constructive play by making plans, creating drawings, and collaborating with others on different designs. Children develop oral language skills as they discuss and solve problems, adjusting their growing constructions.

As children build, they use their creativity to decide what they will construct, what materials they will use, how to refine their project, or what to name the structure. Construction play provides a meaningful way for children to think through possibilities, solve problems, create designs, and implement their ideas with concrete materials.

Natalie (age 4) is constructing with magnetic tiles on the light table, which illuminates the tiles' colors.

Alexa, Marco, and Jason's Story

Alexa (age 4), Marco (age 5), and Jason (age 5) are working in the block center. They discuss what they want to build and decide on a parking garage. As they begin building, they talk about what a parking garage looks like: "It's very tall," "It needs a place where people can pay," "Does it have windows?," and "What about an elevator?" As they proceed with their garage structure, the children change and adjust their design with continual discussion and collaboration. Together they determine that the garage is going to be five stories high with a "humongous" door so that even trucks can get inside the garage.

Reflection

The stimulus for this construction is the new parking garage being built across the street from their school. When their teacher notices that the children are interested in the new structure, she takes the class to the building site several times so they can see the garage in various stages of construction. This firsthand experience helps the children learn some of the details of design and development of the parking garage, knowledge that a small group of children later apply to their own construction. They change features and make adjustments during the building process while collaborating with others involved in the play. During the construction, they integrate what they observe in the building of the garage across the street with other conclusions they reach about how their garage will work (a "humongous" door for trucks), which results in an original design for their parking garage. This play begins with a concrete experience and moves to symbolical representation.

Pretend and Socio-Dramatic Play

During the preschool years, children become increasingly involved in pretend play. They use their imagination to take on roles of other people and different creatures. Socio-dramatic play is a higher level of pretend play that involves pretending (make-believe), using language to communicate ideas, collaborating on decisions, creating intricate story lines and following sequences of events, reinventing the play so it evolves and becomes more complex over time, and using symbols (Piaget 1971; Smilansky and Shefatya 1990; Vygotsky [1930–35] 1978). As children participate in this play, they use creative thinking and develop their social skills as they work with others. They have the freedom to try new approaches, suggest different ideas, and influence others to see their way of thinking. These play experiences develop skills they need now and help prepare them to be creative thinkers, team leaders, and innovators in the future.

A phone call captures the attention of the teacher and begins an interactive conversation.

Anglia, Thomas, and Darnell's Story

Anglia (age 4), Thomas (age 5), and Darnell (age 5) are playing in the camping center that has been set up with a tent, a "campfire" (logs), a small picnic table, and other camping equipment. The three of them are very interested in this center because their families often go hiking, camping, and fishing. Anglia assumes the role of the mother, Darnell is the granddaddy, and Thomas is the inquisitive young child. First they look around the campsite and examine the battery lantern, the cooking utensils, and the blankets. Together they determine what they will cook on the fire for dinner, with suggestions like hot dogs, lasagna, hamburgers, and marshmallows. After some discussion, they realize that lasagna would be difficult to cook on the fire, so they settle on making hot dogs. Granddaddy Darnell suggests they go on a hike before cooking, and they consider which trail to follow. Thomas insists they take the "Big Loop Trail" so they will be back before dark. Before they begin their hike, they put on boots, hats, and gloves. They also decide that they need a flashlight and a first aid kit, just in case. Anglia, with the help of the other two children, collects adhesive bandages, antiseptic wipes, and an ointment-like tube. After hiking around the room, they return to cook dinner, roast marshmallows, and listen to Granddaddy tell a scary story. Finally, they take off their boots and take the lantern inside the tent to rest.

Reflection

These children use their personal experiences with camping to create a rich play scenario where their creative thinking is continually challenged. Each decides the role he or she will take on (role playing). They use camping vocabulary to talk about what they will make for dinner, the trail they will hike, and the equipment they need (language and collaboration). They plan a sequence of events: exploring props, deciding on a meal, hiking the trail, cooking, hearing stories from Granddaddy, and resting (sequence in play). The children were involved in this play episode for 22 minutes (persistence).

Creative Dramatics

Stories, literature, and dramatization provide another avenue for creative development. Reading, telling, or watching stories can inspire children's creativity as they develop a character, add sound effects, act out a sequence of events, or write an original play.

Creative dramatics is appropriate for young children's level of development because it doesn't require memorizing a script or delivering a perfect performance. Rather, in creative dramatics the children select a story to dramatize (either from a book or from their own imaginations), decide what characters they will play, adjust the story line to their own interpretation, informally change the content, and respond extemporaneously to other characters and events in the production. This freedom allows young children to participate in ways that feel comfortable and enjoyable to them. No rehearsal is needed, but some groups like to walk through the story, refine lines, and make other changes that are needed. One group of children might be concerned that the audience will not know when to clap for their performance. After much discussion, they could decide to make a sign that says "Applause" for one child to hold up during their performance. Although props are not needed for creative dramatics, sometimes children want to create an item or a costume that they believe is important for the story: a magic wand, clown shoes, or a pair of sunglasses. These items may help them get into character and enrich the story line.

Maryann's Class's Story

Maryann reads *Giraffes Can't Dance* (2001) to her kindergartners. Written by Giles Andreae and illustrated by Guy Parker-Rees, it is the story of a giraffe named Gerald who is mocked by other animals because he can't dance. After reading the book Maryann asks, "What did you think of the animals that made fun of Gerald?" "I think the animals were really *mean!*" Karl responds. Maryann asks, "Was there a character you really enjoyed besides Gerald?" "Yeah, the cricket!" Sharon claps her hands in excitement. "We need more crickets in the story!" Maya shouts. Building on their responses, Maryann asks, "Would you tell this story in a different way? How would you tell this story?"

After talking with the children about telling the story in a different way, the children ask to hear the story again. Maryann rereads it and then asks the children if they are interested in dramatizing the story and adding some of the suggestions they generated during their discussion. The children are thrilled. Leonardo volunteers to be Gerald, the main character in the story, because he is tall and can dance in zigzag motions, which he happily demonstrates. Amelia wants to be the mouse that appears at the end of the story. Other children choose to be a snake, a dinosaur, a cat, and giant crickets, and each child suggests how he or she would be friendly to Gerald from the beginning and teach him how to dance. Some children decide to be musicians or the audience. In this new version of the story, Gerald is a hero who masters his dance moves with his friends, and all the other animals participate as heroes too.

The jungle animals celebrate the occasion, accompanied by the musicians and cheerful audience members.

Reflection

This story provides many open-ended possibilities for Maryann and the children to implement their own ideas, such as adding new characters, modifying the story line in a way that alters the tone of the original (everyone is helpful and friendly, not "mean"), or including scenes before, during, and at the conclusion of the drama. Sharing a story that contains characters and events that children can add to or alter encourages them to be creative participants. Children enjoy taking ownership of their role or character in the drama when given opportunities to improvise and create stories, characters, or props for use during a presentation. Giving value to every role is a good way to include children of varying talents and abilities and help everyone feel that their ideas and parts are appreciated. In this case, some children wanted to be a musician or a member of the audience, which offered the perfect moment for the teacher to discuss possible roles and explain that performances have performers, people who work backstage with props or sets, an audience, and musicians that accompany the characters' songs or provide music as transitions from one scene to another. An intriguing story that expands into a dramatization invites children's active participation in a language-rich, challenging learning opportunity.

Storytelling: Playing With Narratives

Young children play with language as they experiment with sounds, words, phrases, and stories. As they participate in this verbal play, they begin to understand the power of their language, how they can use it to influence others, and ways to participate in the exchange of telling. Brown and Vaughan (2010) describe storytelling as a unit of human understanding that occupies a central place in early development as children learn.

Children who hear stories read and told will often replicate these literacy experiences. They begin to repeat favorite phrases, imitate gestures, dictate similar stories, and make up their own stories as they gain both an understanding of how stories work and confidence in their creative abilities. As you read and talk about stories, children learn that stories have settings, characters, and a beginning, middle, and end (sequence). This *story sense*, first described by Applebee (1978), helps children develop better story comprehension, retell more complex stories, and create their own original stories.

Meg's Story

As a child, Meg, a Head Start teacher, enjoyed the picture book *Millions of Cats* (1928), by Wanda Gág. She wants to share this story with the children in her classroom. After purchasing a copy of the book from an online used book dealer, she realizes that the illustrations are in black and white and now seemed dated. She wonders if sharing it with her class is a good idea after all. However, she reads the book again and realizes that the story is wonderful, with an intriguing language pattern ("millions, and billions, and trillions of cats") and an important message: If a scrawny cat (and, by extension, other creatures) is taken care of, fed, and loved, it can become a beautiful cat. Meg takes a creative risk. Although she has little experience telling stories, she has heard some wonderful storytellers; so, she reads the story herself many times, rehearses the repetitive pattern, and practices telling it to her family. Finally, she feels ready to tell the story to the children. To her astonishment, they listen intently, repeat the catchy phrases with her, and understand the message. After they discuss the story with her, they want Meg to tell it again.

Several days later, Barthlow (age 4), comes to Meg during snack time and asks if she would like to hear his story. Meg listens to his story attentively, nodding her head during his telling. He tells her the story she had shared with the children, including the repeated pattern of words, but his version is "millions, and billions, and trillions of *rabbits*."

Reflection

Telling the children about her love for this wonderful book when she was around their age creates a powerful connection between Meg and the children. When the book arrives and the illustrations are not colorful, she is faced with a problem, and her solution is to try a different way of sharing the story. This is a new challenge for her, a possible risk that might not work, but she confronts it, prepares the story, and tells it to the children, who are enthusiastic in their appreciation of her storytelling abilities. Hearing, participating in, and enjoying this powerful story told by his teacher inspires Barthlow to think about alternative ways *he* could tell the story and share it with Meg.

Playing With Musical Improvisation, Composition, and Instruments

Many children sing as they play, repeating a song they know or perhaps replacing familiar lyrics with words that match their activity. Other times they add extra musical phrases, new rhythmic patterns, or variations on the melody (improvisation). Some children are able to create original melodies (composition). The sounds from musical wind chimes in a classroom may inspire a child to compose a song. This original song might be expanded, with another child accompanying on rhythm sticks or taking turns singing different words. For example, Jasper, a 3-year-old, jumped from one carpet to another, singing his own original "jump" song. Each time he landed, he said, "jump" and clapped once to make an offbeat. He created a music pattern by jumping and clapping until other children started joining in. They were thrilled to make music (rhythmic patterns) and began pulling other instruments from the baskets on the shelf.

Rhythm instruments can be used to accompany singing, dancing, or recorded music. Children can also build their own musical instruments, which provides further opportunities for them to use creative thinking to produce, identify, differentiate, and manipulate a variety of sounds. Introducing musical vocabulary, such as *soft/loud, fast/slow, high/low,* and *short/long* enriches children's understanding of music components as they begin to attach this terminology to the sounds they hear. An environment with music not only nurtures children's creativity and presents opportunities to explore in another domain, it also encourages children to be active musicians rather than passive listeners (Hildebrandt 1998; Hildebrandt & Zan 2002).

The Impact of Play on the 4Cs

Children need many different play opportunities that support active learning, language development, social functioning, problem solving, and innovative thinking. As you design and provide play environments and materials for the children in your program, think about how play supports the 4Cs introduced in Chapter 1.

Creativity. Will and Elizabeth are playing in the outdoor sand area, and Will suggests the possibility of making a big volcano. Both children look for a large shovel to make the volcano by digging deeper into the sand. They find out quickly that the sand will not hold together or make the tall volcano they want, so Elizabeth suggests wetting the sand. This works, and they bring in more sand and water to make more volcanoes. During this playtime the children experiment with sand and water, suggest ideas, test them out, draw conclusions, and find solutions to their problem.

Communication. There are many opportunities to communicate with others in play, which helps children understand how to share ideas, work together, mentor peers, and reach a decision. In the music center, several 5-year-old children browse through a CD collection displayed by the teacher. They select a musical audiobook recording of *Peter and the Wolf* because they are intrigued by the cover art. While they listen to the various sounds representing animals, they are inspired to accompany the music. "What can we play to sound like the bird?" The children discuss the high sounds of the bird and decide to use the finger cymbals and bells. "What could we use for the wolf? He is mean, big, and loud!" They experiment with woodblocks, a keyboard, and a guiro, but ultimately choose a big drum. After much discussion, they use their musical instruments to accompany the recording. When young children are playing, their communication is focused and meaningful, and it provides immediate, effective feedback.

Collaboration. Children talk, discuss, disagree, and make decisions about their play in construction, socio-dramatic play, and creative dramatics. They listen and adjust their ideas as they collaborate with others. For instance, when a small group of children discusses how to act out "Three Billy Goats Gruff," they discover that three boys want to be the big bad troll. With only five children in the group, what are they to do? After much debate and consideration of alternatives, they decide that their story will have two goats and a three-headed troll who lives under the bridge.

Critical thinking (problem solving). As children play, problems arise that must be solved. A tall structure topples over, and the children wonder, "How can we make the structure more stable?" A computer app is not working. "What do we want it to do, and what can we try?" A puzzle piece is not fitting perfectly. "Where else could it go?" The toy car goes too fast down an incline. "What can we do to make the car run slower?" Some children are upset that they don't get a turn on the new riding toy outdoors. "How can we make sure everyone gets a turn?" Children learn how to work with each other and come up with ways to solve problems.

Play is the source of innovation, providing the ingredients necessary for developing, applying, and modifying ideas. Play activities offer a safe environment for testing scenarios and determining their probability of success. Many business and technology fields recognize that play is a very important source of new ideas, products, and solutions that may keep an organization from become obsolete (Brown & Vaughan 2010). As a teacher, you have an important role—to inspire, encourage, and provide time for play to support the development of creative thinkers.

Reflections

> What opportunities do children have for play in your classroom?

> What types of play do you observe occurring each day? How do these affect the development of creativity?

> When you observe children playing creatively, where are they playing? What are they doing that shows they are thinking creatively?

> How could you provide additional play experiences that support and enrich children's level of development and interest?

> How do you articulate to others the importance of play for children's creative development?

James (age 4) is involved in sensory exploration. He is feeling, pounding, and squeezing clay to determine its properties. Next, he molds and shapes the clay into a form. When a new material is added, it inspires a more complex use of clay and sparks James's imagination.

"My feet are cold. I need to warm them up," says Aysha (age 5) as she uses two bright scarves to create special wrapping socks for her feet.

ibrant collection of clothes, arves, shoes, and hats in the amatic play center stimulates ldren's play and imagination.

io-Dramatic Play: Dress-Up

Sally (age 3) is going to the movie theater wearing an aqua silk skirt and her favorite '50s diner shirt.

Evidence of Creating, Thinking, and Learning

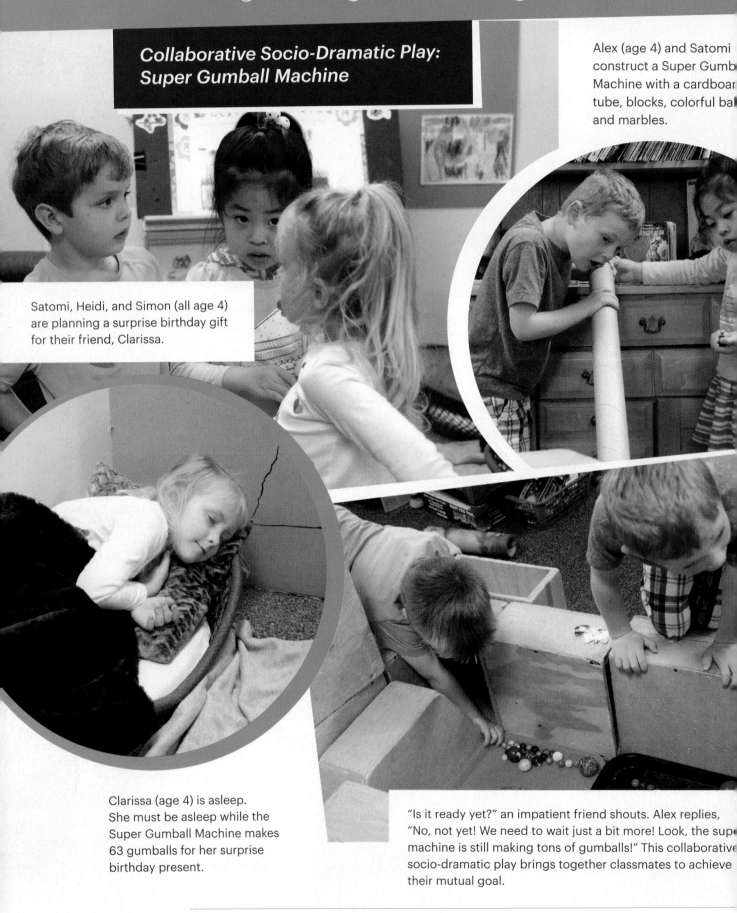

Collaborative Socio-Dramatic Play: Super Gumball Machine

Alex (age 4) and Satomi construct a Super Gumball Machine with a cardboard tube, blocks, colorful balls, and marbles.

Satomi, Heidi, and Simon (all age 4) are planning a surprise birthday gift for their friend, Clarissa.

Clarissa (age 4) is asleep. She must be asleep while the Super Gumball Machine makes 63 gumballs for her surprise birthday present.

"Is it ready yet?" an impatient friend shouts. Alex replies, "No, not yet! We need to wait just a bit more! Look, the super machine is still making tons of gumballs!" This collaborative socio-dramatic play brings together classmates to achieve their mutual goal.

Chapter 7

Extending Thinking With Materials

Tell me and I forget, show me and I remember, involve me and I understand.

—Chinese proverb

The materials you provide for children to explore have a profound influence on their development and learning. To meet a wide range of developmental needs, use your own creativity and imagination to collect eclectic materials for your classroom. Beyond commercially produced items, provide unconventional and natural materials, along with objects, materials, or tools contributed by families or donated by community resources. In addition to having access to an array of materials, children also need sufficient time to explore them so they can ask questions, develop an understanding of how materials can be used and combined in a variety of ways, follow interesting provocations, and return to materials again and again.

Materials should invite play and experimentation, support language development, facilitate social interactions, encourage physical development, and offer choices that spark creativity. Some materials, such as blocks, dress-up clothes, art supplies, and books, should be available throughout the year so children can have sustained, in-depth experiences. Other items can be rotated in and out of the classroom to reflect children's evolving interests, meet their needs for expanded possibilities, and support their learning in specific ways. The materials discussed in this chapter have the potential to draw children into playing, exploring, manipulating, thinking, pretending, and solving problems.

Open-Ended Materials

Open-ended materials, such as blocks, balls, playdough, pipe cleaners, cellophane paper, and buttons, inspire imaginative, inventive play because of their ability to be integrated into different play experiences. The flexibility of these items naturally leads to a fluency of ideas as children transform them to fit their designs and creations. With so many possibilities offered by open-ended materials, children can expand the boundaries of their thinking and develop intriguing creations (Fox & Schirrmacher 2015; Topal & Gandini 1999). Conversely, one-use items have limited possibilities; adding an old coffee maker to the dramatic play center might inspire a child to pretend to make coffee but little else.

Some open-ended materials that can be used in a variety of ways include spools, feathers, and shells.

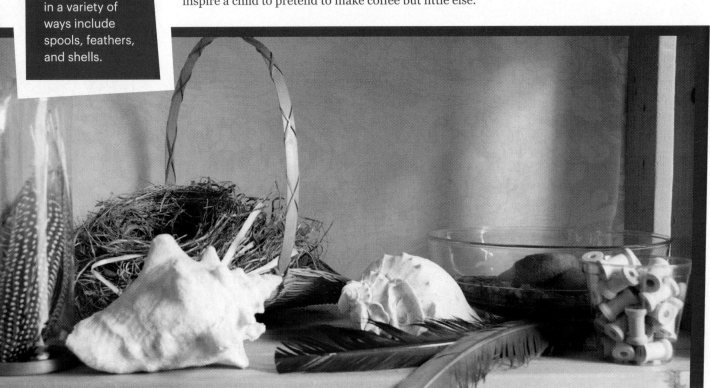

Nurturing Creativity: An Essential Mindset for Young Children's Learning

Wooden blocks are one example of a material that can be used in many ways. Blocks can become a spaceship flying to Mars, part of a barn door, a grand piano, a fence penning in a lion at the zoo, a measuring tool—the possibilities are endless. Block play can be enhanced by adding colorful fabric, aluminum foil, branches or twigs, or pieces of cardboard into the mix. These bonus materials encourage children to combine materials with different properties in innovative ways.

Add a container with various lengths of electric wires, springs, nuts and bolts, colorful ribbons, glittery beads, and pipe cleaners to the art center. Children intrigued by the collection might dump the materials onto a table for closer inspection. By studying each item, they will compare and contrast them and explore their different properties, such as the flexibility of the wires and springs. During this exploratory process, they might begin to think about how they can combine the materials and transform them into an amazing creation.

In addition to having many uses, materials should also be selected to reflect the diversity of children's homes, families, and communities (Epstein 2014). A collection of recycled, unusual items provides hands-on, concrete options that children can relate to or use to put their experiences in context (Isenberg & Durham 2015). Because these open-ended materials are so flexible, they can be included in a variety of classroom centers and used by children with different abilities and interests. The lists in this chapter offer more suggestions for open-ended materials to incorporate in your classroom.

Loose Parts

Loose parts, as first described by British architect Simon Nicholson (1972), are another important part of a creative environment. Nicholson notes that the richness of an environment is affected by the availability of materials that provide interesting connections and challenging combinations. Some examples of loose parts are metal washers, knobs, wooden spools, stones, springs, and gears. Loose parts are distinctive and often include items that children do not commonly examine; for this reason, they provide novel experiences that engage children's interest. Manipulating these unfamiliar items challenges them to think in different ways and generate several ways to use them.

Loose parts are flexible enough to be repeatedly repurposed. This versatility nurtures children's problem-solving abilities as they experiment with a specific use and then transform the materials into another arrangement, design, or possibility (Daly & Beloglovsky 2015). For example, the children in one program are concerned that the class gerbils are bored in their cage and have nothing to play with. Their problem is "How can we help gerbils play?" They discover a piece of fiberglass screen that can be rolled into a tube and cut with scissors. They talk about ways to make the screen stay in the tunnel shape, and after looking through the materials in the invention center, they find some short pieces of copper wire that they twist to connect the sides of the screen together. "But is one tunnel enough?" they wonder. Together they

Redirecting Creativity

If children do not have a collection of interesting, appropriate materials to explore, they will invent things to do, like climbing a bookcase or stacking some blocks to then destroy the structure—over and over again. With a little resourcefulness and no additional materials, the teacher could redirect such creative energy by inviting children to sing and dance to a new song or dramatize a familiar story. If a few additional materials can be obtained, such as dress-up clothes donated by the children's families, the teacher could redirect the children's creativity into a pretend play scenario. One teacher who faced this situation of restless children and limited resources to invest in new materials challenged her class to build a toy with loose parts from the creative reuse center. Some of the children put their creative energy into working together to construct a new toy, which they called a "super bell rattle."

Containers for Collections

Displaying collections in attractive containers in one place helps young children consider their choices more effectively. Containers in a variety of types, textures, and size will further extend their thinking about aesthetically pleasing displays.

> Baskets

> Fruit containers

> Bags (clear plastic, brown paper, cloth, and mesh)

> Sand buckets

> Clear plastic containers, trays, and plates

> Milk jugs or detergent bottles

> Utility carts with storage space

> Shoeboxes and various cardboard boxes

These natural materials include a bird's nest, feathers, and stones displayed in a wicker basket.

determine that three tunnels would be much more fun, so they roll two more pieces of screen into tunnels and attach them together to make what they call a "Gerbils' Play Maze." Over the next few days, they watch as the gerbils scamper in and out of the maze. Their solution worked, and the gerbils were playing.

Natural Materials

Children are mesmerized by natural materials such as water, dirt, sand, and rocks, which they often spend long periods of time examining, experimenting with, moving, and combining. Natural materials can be rotated into the classroom or moved outdoors to extend the opportunities for hands-on learning experiences. Gandini (2005), finding that choosing and arranging natural items is pleasurable for both children and adults, describes the importance of including them in the classroom and studio space or art center. Natural materials provide an avenue to extend and build on what is happening in the physical world. When children and adults have the time to explore and talk about these materials together, their interactions inspire new adventures. As children experiment with putting sand in different containers and sifters, the teacher might describe what is happening or ask the children questions to get them thinking. "I wonder whether this container will hold more sand, or that one . . . what do you think? Why?" Observing a child pouring sand into a sifter, she might ask, "Where do you think the sand is going? What happens when you shake the sifter?"

Here are a few suggested natural materials to add to the classroom:

> Shells and pebbles

> Wood chips and bark pieces

> Stones

> Flowers, leaves, and grass (dried and fresh)

> Branches, twigs, and vines

> Seedpods, pinecones, kernels, acorns, and dried beans

> Nests

> Sand and mud

> Snow and ice

Construction Materials and Tools

To inspire and encourage children's creative constructions, introduce materials that can be used for building, such as

> Electrical wire

> Boxes

> Lumber, such as tree stumps

> Craft sticks

> Cotton swabs

> Tiles

> Gears and components from broken appliances and machines

> Cardboard pieces and tubes

> Small bricks

> Clay

Offer tools for children to use in construction to expand the possibilities of combining, connecting, changing, and refining materials (and their ideas!).

> Paintbrushes

> Pencils, including colored and charcoal

> Markers

> Chalk

> Crayons

> Scissors

> Hammers and screwdrivers

> Rulers and measuring tapes

> Natural and synthetic sponges

> Stapler and staples

> Plastic beakers and/or clear plastic bottles

> Tape (masking, vinyl, plastic, cloth, and duct tape)

> Glue

> Yarn, rope, and fishing line

The Ant Hotel

The teacher introduces sculptures and provides a range of materials for children to use.

The children research sculptures by reading informational books.

In a small group, the children plan their project (an "Ant Hotel"), figure out how to implement it, and make changes when needed.

Teacher: You want a hotel for ants? How did you decide you wanted it to be something for ants?

Boy: Because the ants don't have a house. We built this for them to have one. They don't have hands to build it.

Teacher: How did you know that the ants would like this?

Girl: Well, we just thought it was better.

Teacher: So what made you plan that?

Boy: Our brain!

The Ant Hotel is complete with playground and water slides.

Making Sounds

Children are fascinated by objects and toys that make sound or can be used to create music by shaking, tapping, and jingling them. Provide sound-producing materials in the music center to capture the interest of children in small group projects or during whole group time. These materials can also be added to the science area so children can explore sound vibration (physics), investigate differences in pitch, and observe how sound is made. Instruments that can be plucked or tuned, such as guitars and ukuleles, are great for exploring sound vibration, and a dulcimer allows for experimentation with pitch by pressing the space close to the frets.

Natalie (age 4) and Alex (age 3) listen to the sounds they can make using a tin can and a rubber band. They place the rubber bands around the opening of the can and pluck them. Natalie notices that when she puts two rubber bands across the opening in an X shape, it sounds muffled. "Why does mine not sound like yours, Alex?" Natalie wonders. Alex has two parallel rubber bands across the opening and they sound beautiful. The more he stretches them, the higher the sound rises. Soon Natalie notices that the X of the rubber band is muffling the sound. She removes one of the rubber bands, and the remaining one sounds just like Alex's. Extending their investigation, they use various sizes of cans and discover how rubber bands sound when wrapped around a cup made of bamboo and a plastic container. Explorations with sound are a wonderful way to help children question, problem-solve, and experiment with variables. Chord instruments and rhythm sticks are good options, but be sure to present the children with a variety of instruments and sound-producing materials that they can play and investigate.

While most children are fascinated by sounds and music, some prefer less auditory stimulation. Watch for cues and listen to their words as they describe their interest in the sounds or their desire to soften the sounds. Sensitive children may cover their ears or move away from an area with noise that is distracting or uncomfortable for them. You might provide earmuffs or headphones so those children can adjust the volume or gradually introduce new sounds (Isbell & Isbell 2008).

Here are a few of the many items that can be used to make sounds.

> Bells of various sizes, preferably uncolored so children need to listen to identify differences in pitch

> Metal piping cut into different lengths (file to smooth all sharp edges)

> Bolts, screws, and washers

> Mallets made with dowel rods and felt, yarn, wood, or rubber

> Large nails and other metal items

> Bamboo and wood

> Embroidery hoops to combine with other materials to make hanging mobiles or chimes

> Tin cans (remove the entire lid and leave no sharp edges)

> Rubber bands

> Clear containers and hard plastic bottles with small items to put inside to make a shaker (sand, tiny shells, or pebbles)

> Clay flower pots

> Kitchen utensils, like whisks and spoons

> Balloons with open end cut off and stretched over the openings of tin cans to create a drumhead

> PVC pipes

> Cardboard boxes

> Tongue depressors and craft sticks

Connectors

Means to combine or join materials is key to many projects children take on. Materials can be combined and attached using

> Glue
> Clamps and clips
> Nails and hammer/screws and screwdriver
> Wires (aluminum, steel, and nylon-covered)
> Tape (masking and double-sided)
> Cords, strong yarn, and ribbon
> Dowel rods
> Clear plastic tubing
> Stapler and staples
> Adhesive-backed paper
> Clothespins (wood and plastic)
> Strips of fabric
> Chenille sticks
> Rubber bands
> Twist ties

Display Materials

Children are drawn to eye-catching materials, arrangements, and displays. Possible materials that may appeal to children for displaying or enhancing their work include

> Parchment paper
> Aluminum foil
> Brown shipping paper
> Butcher paper
> Computer paper
> Construction paper

> Wrapping paper with various designs, colors, textures, and transparency
> Envelopes
> Eyedroppers and basters
> Baking cups
> Buttons and beads
> Picture frames

> Wallpaper scraps
> Costume jewelry (with sharp parts removed)
> Fabric (translucent, textured, and soft)
> Foam insulation
> Shower curtains
> Tablecloths

Technology Tools

In our world of expanding technology, children need appropriate, interactive tools that they can control and that will respond to their original ideas.

Apps. With so many software applications available on computers, tablets, and smartphones, it is critical to choose those that are appropriate. Select apps that allow children to explore the digital medium and that respond to their actions without confining their thinking or limiting their options. Interacting with the children as they use the apps or encouraging children to use them together will enhance their learning and enjoyment.

Digital camera. Digital cameras are used to document the creation process by recording ideas and activities. They are essential in the development of documentation panels that provide evidence of the learning that happens during project work or focused study.

Drawing and painting software. Art software must allow the child to control the design. Rather than replacing experiences with crayons, markers, paints, and other concrete materials, open-ended software should be seen as an additional way to create.

Light table. Light tables originated as an architect's tool, but they are also used in Reggio Emilia–inspired programs. For children, they illuminate another perspective of materials, such as a building of colored blocks, designs on a plastic sheet, or oils and paints in a clear pie pan.

Overhead projector. This is another tool that allows children to see their work from a different perspective. Children can draw, design, write, or explore with markers and colored blocks on clear transparency sheets or cellophane paper. Used overheads can be found cheaply online—or perhaps at the back of a storage closet.

Books and Audiobook Recordings

You probably already have a collection of one of the most important materials for stimulating curiosity and creativity: books! There are many wonderful books that inspire or challenge children to come up with unique ideas, think in flexible ways, ponder questions, solve dilemmas, and venture into new territories. Stories can simply be enjoyed together, or they can be used as a jumping-off point for imaginative ideas and activities. The following are just a few interesting titles to share with children.

What Do You Do With an Idea? (2014), by Kobi Yamada and Mae Besom As a child's wild, wonderful idea grows, so does the child's confidence.	***Little Blue and Little Yellow*** (1959), by Leo Lionni Little blue and little yellow are best friends, and when they hug one day, they discover they make something new—green!	***Dreaming Up: A Celebration of Building*** (1996), by Christy Hale Parallels are drawn between children's creations and famous architecture through this collection of poetry, illustrations, and photographs.
The Artist Who Painted a Blue Horse (2011), by Eric Carle An artist uses his imagination to paint the world as he sees it.	***Duck! Rabbit!*** (2009), by Amy Krouse Rosenthal and Tom Lichtenheld This book is a fun take on an optical illusion that teaches children about differences in perspective.	***It Looked Like Spilt Milk*** (1947), by Charles G. Shaw This classic story shows how a little imagination opens up a world of possibilities.
The Big Orange Splot by (1977), Daniel Manus Pinkwater A man's house is splashed with orange paint, which inspires him to paint the rest of his house in a very different way.	***Beautiful Oops*** (2010), by Barney Saltzberg Discover how every mistake is a chance to make something wonderful.	***Do You Know Which Ones Will Grow?*** (2011), by Susan A. Shea and Tom Slaughter A nonfiction book that illustrates the differences between living and nonliving things and encourages problem solving.
Nana in the City (2014), by Lauren Castillo A boy is scared of the noise and crowds of the city until Nana sews him a special cape that makes him brave.	***Christina Katerina and the Box*** (1971), by Patricia Lee Gauch and Doris Burn Christina Katerina discovers that if you use your imagination, a box can be anything you want it to be.	***Imogene's Antlers*** (1985), by David Small A little girl wakes up to find that she has sprouted antlers overnight. How does she handle this unexpected development?

Materials Are Important in All Domains

It is important to look for materials that can spark creative thinking across multiple domains, including math, science, literacy, the visual arts, drama/theater, and music/movement.

Mathematical Thinking

Young children need to experiment with concrete materials as they build a foundation for understanding math concepts. Manipulating and arranging items helps them grasp basic concepts, such as one-to-one correspondence, counting, sorting, making patterns, sequencing, and comparing parts to the whole. A pre-K teacher brings a collection of children's shoes, including sneakers, sandals, boots, and slippers, into the classroom for the children to explore. As they explore, she asks questions to get them thinking about similarities and differences, such as "Do you have any shoes like these?," "How are they similar?," "How are they different?," and "How can you put them in groups?" The teacher observes and documents their various ways of classifying, focusing on how each child thinks and reaches conclusions. Open-ended materials provide children with many opportunities to use and refine their skills while they work at their own pace and select the items that interest them. These choices give children some control over the activity and make experiences more meaningful.

Scientific Exploration

To help children investigate science concepts effectively, provide open-ended materials that they can manipulate, combine, separate, and change in a variety of ways. Encourage them to make predictions about what will happen, experiment with variables to see if their ideas are supported, and think over the results. Providing a supportive environment where children can safely learn through experimentation based on their observations and predictions will ignite children's ideas and give them the opportunity to solve problems on their own. Children learn to be scientists by investigating real problems and engaging in a process of thinking and acting. During this process there will be successes and frustrations, including making mistakes and trial and error. Offering sufficient time, challenges, or additional thought-provoking materials helps children deepen their understanding of scientific concepts. Enrich children's ideas by integrating materials carefully and posing open-ended questions that encourage multiple answers and unconventional thinking.

Literacy

Share a wide variety of books with children—wordless books, books with eye-catching illustrations, informational books, predictable books, books of poetry, alphabet and number books, board books, pop-up books, big books, and ebooks. When you read with children, put yourself into it. Use a scary voice, a silly voice, animated expressions—whatever helps make a story come alive. Savor special words you come across. Spark exploration and experimentation with a collection of unusual writing tools in the writing/illustrating center, such as colored chalk, wax crayons, tempera paint, pen and ink, sponge brushes, and glitter glue. Provide materials for children to create their own books, such as cardboard, pipe cleaners, hole punchers, rings, fabric, foam pieces, yarn, ribbons, and paper of different colors, textures, sizes, and shapes. Display child-made books in the classroom library and other areas to be enjoyed by the authors, other children and teachers, and families.

The Visual Arts

Give children many opportunities to experiment with two- and three-dimensional compositions. Provide materials of varied color, texture, design, and construction, and offer activities that encourage children to work together in small groups or as a class. New materials and methods will encourage problem solving, flexible thinking, and collaboration. Be creative in what you provide for children to create with! (See Chapter 3 for a more detailed discussion on providing visual art experiences for children.)

Drama and Theater

Drama and language are enhanced when you add a stage, a microphone, and items that can serve as costumes, set pieces, and props. In this area of the arts, children collaborate on their plans for a play by making decisions about characters, developing a plot, and gaining confidence in their ability to communicate their ideas in different ways. They might design a backdrop, invitations, and a billboard for their performance. Books that have an easy-to-follow story line, a few characters, and a lot of action can stimulate children to dramatize, retell, and recreate their own version of the story. (Chapter 3 provides more suggestions for drama and theater activities for children.)

Music and Movement

Children respond to music with their bodies, voices, and emotions. They learn how to distinguish sounds, pauses, rhythms, melodies, and phrases. Instruments will enrich these experiences, encourage experimentation, heighten the children's interest, and increase their enjoyment. The addition of unique materials can challenge them to think in new ways, distinguish different sounds and create new ones, and build their confidence as they discover various ways to make music and sounds interesting. Music invites children to move their bodies to the rhythm and melody. Children often begin by imitating each other's movements, but the teacher can encourage more creative improvisation by commenting on a child or children who are moving in more original ways. This encourages other children to also try different ways of moving and expressing their feelings.

These girls (all age 5) are discussing the characters, sequence, and ending of their play.

Supporting Children's Use of Creative Materials

The development of self-worth is a significant need for children. Materials that slightly challenge their thinking provide ways for children to problem-solve, be successful, and collaborate with others—all of which builds and reinforces their belief that they are capable and creative. You play an integral part in children's cognitive and emotional development, especially when they are struggling to find a potential solution to a problem, such as using a pulley to lift and transport items to another area. Instead of offering a quick solution, first simply be there with the child to observe and acknowledge the problem. If a child does need your help solving the problem, decide what kind of help to offer. A child who can solve problems independently or facilitated by adults will develop confidence in her ability to tackle other challenges. Activities that allow for multiple methods and outcomes can provide successful experiences that will also build children's confidence in their growing abilities. The creative process provides a safe way for young children to explore, experiment, problem-solve, and learn about their capabilities (Edwards 2010).

Open-ended materials provide a way for children to be successful and work at their own level. For children who need additional challenges, more difficult problems, and the opportunity to set their imagination free, open-ended materials offer what they need to extend their thinking. Encourage children to use materials that support their strengths and expand their thinking. If a child is overwhelmed by too many options and finds it difficult to focus, limit the choices available to him at first to make decision making more manageable. Keep workspaces well organized and spacious; a crowded area with too many items may distract children and hinder them from carrying through with their ideas.

This simple space provides a calming place for children to think and work.

When to Add Materials

Observe the children's involvement, specific needs, and developing ideas to decide what materials to add and when. As you watch and listen to children, you will determine if their play is in the exploring stage or if it needs additional stimulation or scaffolding to move to more complex play. It may be as simple as adding a container that has a collection of small figures. At other times, you might need to identify a specific item that would extend the activity. For example, when a child examines a pinecone, providing a magnifying glass may be just the spark needed for a more in-depth examination.

There are other ways of supporting and extending a child's thinking—for example, by talking with him about his work and making suggestions. This scaffolding may spark new ideas or move his thinking in new directions. For example, you might say, "I see you are twisting a wire around these pieces of wood. Tell me what this does," "Are there other ways you might put the two pieces together?," or "It looks like there are no more boards to add to your piece. I wonder if there is something else in the room you could use?" Some children, especially those who are visually or tactually sensitive, may find it difficult to sort through a large group of items to decide what they need. Finding the balance between enough and too much comes from careful observation and awareness of the children's work, the signs of overload, and the frustration that occurs when additional materials are needed.

Each time you add a new material, the children will want to explore, manipulate, and examine it thoroughly before using it in a project, invention, or creation. Recognize this first step and provide the time needed for this essential part of the learning experience. Once the children have completed their careful examination, they will be able to focus on using the new material, tool, or prop in more complex ways.

Too Much Stuff!
Storing Materials

One of the first steps in many early childhood classrooms is decluttering. Often we hear teachers say of an item, "I might need it someday!" But the problem with keeping everything is finding it when you need it. A careful appraisal of all materials in the storage space and throughout the classroom will help determine which items to keep and which must be discarded or given away. When the remaining items are organized, the areas can function more effectively. Begin by scheduling a workday with other teachers and volunteers to focus on eliminating any materials that have not been used for a long time. During this process, you might find things you didn't know you had that could be great additions to your classroom (Isbell & Evanshen 2012).

How items are stored and displayed influences how they are used. Items that are visible and accessible to children will be used more frequently. Clearly label materials with pictures and words in English and children's home languages. Transparent hanging shoe organizers allow children see their choices and return materials back to their designated places. Other storage possibilities include stackable clear containers, wire hampers with wheels, and woven baskets. These visual organizers allow children to make independent choices, follow through with selections, enhance their problem-solving skills, and enrich their play or project.

Clear, labeled storage boxes can be put in a closet or storage area.

Stocking and Rotating Materials

Have you ever seen an early childhood classroom that had enough storage? Where can you put any new materials? How can you rotate things in and out of the space? How can you conceal things that are not in use? It is helpful to keep some materials available that are high interest, flexible, or favorites of the children. This continuity of materials helps maintain an emotionally safe, consistent place that includes choices they love.

On the other hand, when the same materials remain in a classroom for a long time, children become habituated to their existence and no longer see, select, or use these items. Throughout the year and in different areas of the classroom, rotate some items out and replace them with new ones. For instance, the excitement is evident when a box of unusual dress-up items is opened and displayed in the dramatic play area. Children try on an artist's beret or colorful feather boa and look at themselves in the full-size mirror. These items provide a creative spark for new avenues of play and interaction.

Developmentally appropriate, open-ended materials give children the freedom to experiment, make choices, and follow their own interests. Introducing novel items, intriguing materials, and challenging possibilities encourage creative thinking and collaboration as children investigate their properties and ponder options. Observe children's selection, use, and adaptations of materials to gain insight into their thinking and interests. Then use this information to further enrich the environment.

An environment that supports and sustains children's creative thinking will evolve and change throughout the year, but it will also contain basic elements that are continually high interest. Careful observation and examination of children and their creative work will help you determine the appropriate balance of familiar and novel materials.

Reflections

> Take photographs of the different areas of your classroom and use this to help determine how children see your space. Ask a colleague for ideas and input about the areas.

> Think about the materials you have in your classroom. What open-ended items do you have? What new materials could you collect that will spark creative thinking?

> How can you store materials so that they are easily accessible or rotated in and out of the classroom? What are some novel ways you might display items?

> Select a book that relates to creativity and share it with the children. What questions can you pose to capture their interest? How might you expand the experience with follow-up activities? Try some out.

This basket is filled with balls of many sizes, colors, and textures.

Edward watches as Lydia (age 5) examines two balls from the basket. One is translucent and the other is opaque. Lydia exclaims, "It looks like a crystal ball!"

When allowed to explore the balls on her own, Lydia discovers a unique way of sorting the balls: by smell. This demonstrates the importance of respecting children's curiosity and their unique ways of thinking and gathering information.

Lydia shares this idea—and smell—with her friend Ryan.

Lydia wonders what is inside the translucent ball.

Ryan (age 5) figures out that this ball has a light inside, which is activated by being dropped on the table.

Ryan discovers that putting a table tennis ball inside a basket and setting it in motion makes a delightful sound.

Lydia casts light onto a large pink ball. Her face brightens when she finds the solution. "Look, it's shining!"

Michelle (age 5) explores different ways to play the Japanese pellet drum. Here, she is rubbing her hands together to make the beads strike the drumheads.

With this African percussion instrument, Michelle finds that she can produce sounds by tapping it on her hand.

Michelle is experimenting with a kalimba, which leads to her discovery of how to pluck.

Michelle plucks the strings of a ukulele.

Chapter 8

Displaying and Documenting Children's Work

Documentation can serve to illuminate the thinking, a change in thinking that occurred, what was learned or not learned, the evolution of the behavior, questioning, maturity, responses, and opinions.

—Julianne Wurm, *Working in the Reggio Way: A Beginner's Guide for American Teachers*

In environments where creative thinking is cherished, children's works, both ongoing and complete, are prominently displayed. Many early childhood programs have traditionally displayed only the final products of children's efforts. In programs that also value the *process* of creating, displays include documentation (written and visual records) of the whole process—the project's initial question, the steps used, the children's collaboration, and hurdles they overcame. Rather than highlight just one part of the process (the result), displays accompanied by documentation showcase the evolution of an idea over time. Whether they focus on a group painting project, an individual child's time and effort creating an invention, a story drawn by a child and accompanied by squiggled symbols, or a complex structure crafted with tools, displays should be carefully planned, attractively presented, and a meaningful representation of the progression of children's thought processes and narratives.

The Display Process

How can we best display children's work to genuinely reflect their learning and creativity? How can teachers demonstrate their own creativity when displaying children's plans, paintings, sculptures, experiments, conversations, constructions, and inventions? Below we explore the steps to developing an effective display of children's work.

Step 1: Evaluate the Space

Determine what areas are available for displays and how you can use them to share the children's work. Consider these questions:

> What do you see first when you enter your setting? What tone or message is conveyed?

> What areas might best showcase displays that demonstrate the development of a story or project and focus primarily on the process?

> Are unused spaces, such as hallways, corners, or bathroom walls, possibilities?

> How can you use the windows, ceiling, and doors to effectively vary the height and background of displays?

> How can light and shadow (both natural and artificial) play supportive roles in the display?

In this hallway filled with light and shadow, children's work can be exhibited at a variety of heights. Each piece is accompanied by a photograph of the artist.

> How can you replace or remove objects and furniture around the display call attention to the children's work?

Carefully plan the display so it invites engagement, examination, and appreciation of the children's work. Have some displays at a comfortable

Natural materials, a wooden table, framed pictures, and documentation of children's work are incorporated into this display.

height for adults and others that are also visible and accessible to the children so they can admire each other's work.

Step 2: Select Items to Display

Once you identify areas best suited to display the children's work, select the items you want to display in those spaces. As you decide what to display, ask yourself some questions:

> Do the displays reflect children's creative abilities, such as skillful or interesting use of brush, color, objects, ideas, or expressions?

> Does the work demonstrate children's knowledge, skills, experience, and learning?

> Do the displays include children's narratives about their work?

Including the words children use to describe or talk about their work enhances the quality of a display and provides authentic, evidence-based documentation of their thought processes.

You can also ask children what they would like to put on display. Inquire why a child has chosen a certain work—you might be surprised by his explanation or perspective. Involving children in the selection process provides them with an opportunity to self-evaluate, express themselves, and participate in decision making, which makes them feel that their opinions are valued and respected.

Remember that selecting work to display is not about choosing what adults would consider lovely, polished, or exemplary, but showcasing children's techniques, processes, and learning.

Step 3: Look at the Display and Determine What Is Needed

Once the space, the items, and their arrangements are determined, look at the display and decide if it communicates the intended message or tells the complete story. Sometimes this leads to removing some items because it is difficult to follow the sequence. At other times, a more detailed narrative, additional labels, or further explanation about the materials and process may be needed to help the viewer understand the work and the thinking behind it. Rather than including every child's work at the same time, consider rotating them over time.

With fewer items to demand their attention, viewers can dedicate more focus and appreciation to each child's creation. Be flexible when creating the display; arrangements can be developed while a project is still in progress or once it's complete depending on what works best in a particular circumstance. Beautiful, effective displays require ongoing decision making, problem solving, and creative thinking.

What Is Documentation?

The term *documentation* is derived from the idea that engineers and programmers record their thoughts and processes in formal writing, such as in software manuals. In many fields, including medicine, technology, engineering, art, and business, documentation is used as a method of assessment. Supervisors may document a process or product by evaluating the work delivered by employees. Teachers, too, use documentation when assessing or developing a portfolio to share children's academic progress or project work with families, administrators, and other professionals.

Beyond evaluating children's work, documentation is used to capture their thinking processes. Through documentation, children's voices and actions are chronicled and collected by the teacher in written accounts, photographs, audio recordings, or videos. As teachers work alongside the children and facilitate their activities, they observe and record children's words and actions as they create, reflect, and collaborate. While documenting, teachers are actively seeking relevant, informative, or communicative evidence that serves as an "indispensable tool for educators in constructing positive experiences for children and in facilitating professional growth and communication for adults" (Gandini & Goldhaber 2001, 124). Documentation makes children's learning and creative processes more visible, which helps inform teachers' and families' understanding of children's development, individual contributions, and thought processes.

Documentation panels—presentation boards showing project artifacts or evidence of children's learning—provide a powerful addition to the classroom environment, and composing one can be an exciting and collaborative process. Partner with coteachers or volunteers to capture the ongoing process, observing children's actions, listening to and writing down their language, taking pictures, posing questions, securing the needed materials, and interpreting their work.

The benefits of documenting children's work are numerous. Since careful observation is necessary for effective documentation, you learn a great deal about the children through this process. As you record exchanges between the children, you gain specific evidence about each child's language and thinking. You might discover, for example, that Guillermo, who is often quiet during group times, uses an extensive vocabulary to describe his thought process about something he created. You'll also observe children's social skills—for example, as Tyree explains to Jonathan how to attach a wooden piece to his sailboat. Sometimes their actions speak for them instead, such as when Mel holds a piece of copper structure while Genevieve inserts tiny round pieces of washers on top. Aside from learning what the children are constructing, you can use documentation to help them make decisions about extending the work and identifying future projects. The documentation process gives you opportunities to refine your questioning skills and scaffold children's thinking (Helm & Katz 2011).

The Beginning Steps of Documentation

As with any teaching technique, there is no single approach to documentation. You might begin by sitting beside a child, attentively listening to him, and capturing the thoughts he expresses during the activity. Perhaps a child needs some privacy to be creative; if so, move on to the next child, or sit back and observe that child from a distance. It is important to recognize that creative minds, whether children or adults, need space and time to focus. Consider whether it would be more effective to let a child work on her own or if you should intervene with effective questioning to better understand her thinking (Fusco 2012). Sometimes, children need silence to continue the flow of creative ideas, while on other occasions, intentional questions may trigger another idea or direct them to new possibilities (Csikszentmihalyi 2009).

It is more efficient (and manageable) to focus on and collect information from individual children or small groups rather than the entire class at the same time. Keep notepads, clipboards, sticky notes, pens, or pencils on hand to record the children's comments (both amusing and serious) and insightful conversations. Including explanations in the children's own words adds clarification to the documentation. You can also use technology, such as video and audio recording devices, tablets, digital cameras, computers, and smartphones, to document a project. When using a video recording device, the equipment should be set up on a tripod to stabilize it for higher quality recordings and to keep your hands free to take notes while you observe and listen to the children. High-quality microphones are more likely to capture direct quotes from children. When you take photographs and record videos, try different angles. For example, take pictures from the children's perspective for unique results.

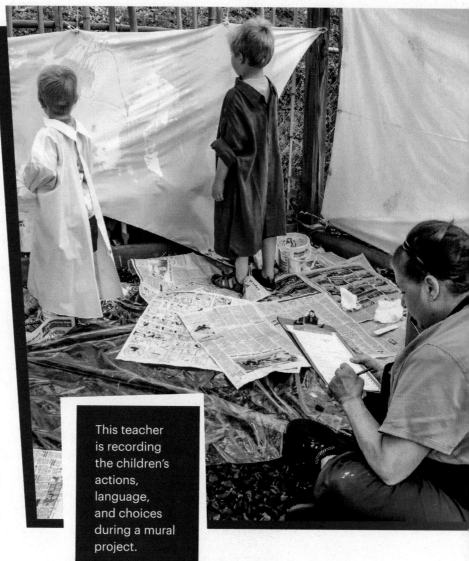

This teacher is recording the children's actions, language, and choices during a mural project.

A Preschool Teacher's Thoughts on Documentation

Ann, an experienced teacher of 4- and 5-year-olds in a Reggio Emilia–inspired program, reveals her approach to documentation in an interview conducted via email on April 3, 2015.

How do you choose what to document? What triggers you to document?

I am prepared to document at any time. If I have set up a provocation, I have my tools (sticky notes, camera, mobile phone) ready to document, but I also keep my mobile phone accessible while interacting with the children. I also take time after a provocation or at midday to sit and reflect on what has happened that morning. I write down the children's dialogue, what they were interested in, how their thinking has been extended, etc. I use the children's drawings, artwork, and writing samples as pieces of documentation as well. As far as what triggers the need, I am aware that the need to document can arise at *any* time during the day.

Do you plan or prepare your documentation ahead of time?

When I enter the classroom in the morning, I have paper, a pen, and my mobile phone with me. The paper I use to document is folded in half. One side I use for children's words and actions. The other side I use to record what I am thinking as I am observing them. I move back and forth and photograph often. I use the photographs to self-reflect about the happenings of the day, as well as for the documentation panels and children's assessment. Sometimes I write down a stream of conversation between children, and other times I ask questions and record the children's answers.

How do you decide when to use a camera, mobile phone, tablet, video camera, or any other recording devices?

I use the camera on my mobile phone. I take photos during the day to document social interactions, children's thinking process, and evidence of the children's progress. I have used an audio recording device for my own reflective practice. I have a long commute home. I often talk into an audio recorder to reflect on my day and record future plans.

What do you have on your mind while using a camera to take pictures of the children's actions?

There are times I use photographs of the children working and planning. I share these photos with the children at a class meeting to help them reflect on their work. I also use the photos to print and post quickly in the room, so we can refer to them to help children extend their thinking on a project. I sometimes take photos from the child's perspective while helping the child and myself reflect on the work that is being done. I take photos to include in portfolio work that is used for assessment purposes. These photos are used as evidence that a child has achieved a developmental milestone. I take photos that I know I will use in a daily reflection, which are also emailed to families to keep them involved in the happenings in our classroom. I also take photographs to use specifically in documentation panel work.

Ann's responses offer insight into how documentation is an ongoing thinking process. She clearly shows that documenting children's work takes preparation, practice, reflection, and—most of all—creativity.

Moving Forward

Many teachers take wonderful pictures and notes throughout the day, but those visual records are often buried and forgotten among thousands of other pictures on a computer hard drive or a mobile device. A more productive way to deal with photographs and narratives is to work on the documentation while it is occurring. If documentation accumulates, schedule time to dig out and systemize it. The notes and anecdotal records you have taken during the experience will guide you in organizing children's work and its chronological process.

To organize records, consider the following:

› Write the children's names while recording their dialogue and ideas.

› Number the order or sequence of the project's progression.

> Note the start and end dates of the project.

> Take notes on each step in the process and how it contributes to the conclusion. If possible, also take at least one photo at each step as a visual record.

In the beginning, you might make many mistakes, feel frustrated, and need to make adjustments. Do not be discouraged—the road to creative documentation is long but rewarding when accomplished and shared with others.

Arriving at the Final Step

The final step in documentation happens after you've collected all notes, videos, transcripts, photographs, and children's works you will use in a display. A workroom or designated space in your classroom can be used to assemble the pieces aesthetically, keeping in mind the viewers and the location where you will place the display.

Begin by visually drafting your ideas for the layout, organization, and design on paper. Invite the children to help you arrange their items, as it will be a collaborative way to demonstrate what you and your children value. There may be some adjustment to your assumptions as the children help you refine the documentation. Together, you can create a wonderful documentation display that captures children's words and ideas, demonstrates their thinking, and celebrates a mutual accomplishment. With time, you will use a variety of forms, styles, and approaches in your documentation methods. Your continuing experimentation and research will ultimately lead to displays that tell engaging stories.

Transition: Your Journey From Documentation to Display

Displaying work that reflects children's ideas and their thought processes requires a great deal of planning. Incorporating documentation into your early childhood environment is a long quest, filled with experimentations, reflections, perspective taking, trial and error, and successes. You are not just filling up space or making the environment attractive. As when learning any new technique, time is needed to gain information, refine your skills, and experiment with varied methods of design and implementation. It may help to see other teachers' documentation, visit museums and galleries for inspiration, or find resource books and websites that will spark your thinking. During this transitional stage of the developmental process, begin implementing new methods, including more descriptions, and developing ways to make children's thought processes more visible. Recognize and understand that while these first efforts might be rudimentary, they demonstrate that you are trying new approaches and striving to provide more complex information and insights into children's thinking.

What Documentation and Displays Communicate

To children. Documenting and displaying children's work communicate to them that their ideas are important and respected. Invite the children to participate in this process as creative collaborators, encouraging them to suggest which of their works should be displayed, how, and where. A child may want his work to be hung upside down, on the ceiling of the hallway, as a mural with other paintings, or as part of a pattern or sequence you had not considered. Children can also take part in selecting or creating their own frames. Seeing the careful

This attractive arrangement includes a live plant, soft lighting, and a canvas painting.

Three-dimensional creations challenge teachers to thir about new ways of displaying children's work.

attention being dedicated to their display will fill them with pride. A display might contain the child's name and a description of the project in their own words. Another presentation may outline the developmental process of the child's work from beginning to conclusion.

To families. Families want to know what their children are thinking and learning when they participate in early childhood programs. Displays can effectively convey this information and often include significant details about the children's language, involvement, and development. The adults in a child's life will be eager to see pictures, projects, and stories contributed by their child and discuss those experiences with their child. Some of these interactions may stimulate further study or research related to the display or collection, such as continuing the project at home together. You can also regularly share children's work with their families through newsletters, a class blog, and videos.

To classroom visitors and the community. When a visitor enters your program, they will form an impression about the environment based on what they observe. If they see a homelike atmosphere decorated with attractive displays of children's artwork, they may conclude that this is a nurturing place that supports children's emotional development and creative thinking. They will see creations made by children using personally selected colors and unusual materials, like an abstract design on an enormous canvas that the class made together using paint, brushes, silver duct tape, and masking tape. A collaborative, unconventional masterpiece like this one displayed in the entrance of the program intrigues visitors and invites them to more closely inspect the unpredictable combination of materials. Be prepared to articulate to parents and visitors that the documentation and any final products they see—which may not seem very attractive by adult standards—represent the children's own ideas and thinking over an extended period of time rather than their imitation of an adult's model.

Some children may want to tell their families and visitors about their contribution to a work and, if encouraged, they may also share the meaning they attach to their representations. Visitors might see children working in small groups on projects like creating robots, framing pictures, or using mapping to develop a plan to solve a math problem involving spatial reasoning. All of these displays and activities communicate to visitors that important creating and learning is taking place and that children are active participants in their learning.

Reflections

> What displays have you completed that were attractive and well organized? What elements did you include and where did you place the display?

> What could you add to displays to help viewers understand how children think creatively and solve problems in your classroom?

> What tools do you need to help you better document children's creative actions and words?

> Identify an interest that children recently expressed. Begin taking notes of the language children use, questions they pose, and experiences that may build on the investigation. Use your recording tools to document this process through each step.

> Design and implement a documentation panel, complete with photographs, provocations, narratives, paintings, and examples of children's thinking.

September 3 – 10:45 a.m.

Ana draws the children's attention [to] the sunflowers' petals, the seeds [in the] heads, and the height of the stem[s].

Carla: "The flower looks round, ju[st like] the sun!"

Tom: "It feels prickly!"

The children in Ana's class walk to the playground every day, passing the sunflower plants that are growing bigger and bigger. They wonder, inquire, and make predictions about the height of the flowers.

Tom (age 5): "These sunflowers are growing to three thousand and five hundred feet tall!"

James (age 5): "These sunflowers are as tall as Alexandra!" *(Alexandra is the tallest child in the class.)*

Carla (age 4): "The sunflowers are eight leaves high." *(Carla counted the leaves on the sunflower's stem.)*

Max (age 4): "We need to use a small box with a thingy that pulls out with numbers on it." *(Max is thinking of a measuring tape.)*

September 4 – 9:15 a.m.

Ana cuts the stem and brings a sunflower into the classroom, propping it up on a tall shelf so the children can investigate its height.

Tom: "Wow, it's GIGANTUOS!"

Ana: "How tall do you think the sunflower plant is?"

How tall are our Sunflowers?

Tom: 3500 ft

James: 65 ft.

Carla: 89 ft.

Max: 7 ft.

September 4 – 9:30 a.m.

Because the children are posing questions about the height of the sunflower, Ana develops a prediction chart to record the children's estimations (shown at left).

Ana provides a variety of measuring instruments for the children to explore and measure with, including a ruler, a yardstick, a measuring tape, linking cubes, yarn, and ribbon. After they finish measuring, the children develop a new understanding of the height of the sunflower. Now they suggest more accurate measurements, in the range of 6 to 9 ft.

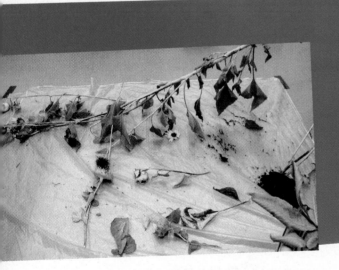

September 5 – 9:00 a.m.

The children are interested in exploring the parts of the sunflower more closely. Ana breaks apart the stem, the head, and the leaves for the children to investigate, feel, smell, and examine in closer detail.

Carla: "I like the feel of this leaf! It is smooth."

Max: "The small sunflowers have teeny tiny seeds!"

September 5 – 9:15 a.m.

With a variety of tools to aid their investigation, the children look through magnifying glasses, observe the flower's reflection on the mirror, and dissect the flower head.

Max: "Look at all these tiny seeds! They are packed together! How many are there?"

Carla: "There are hundreds!"

September 8 – 9:30 a.m.

Ana: "How can you represent a sunflower with paint on paper?"

Natalie (age 5): "You need yellow, black, and maybe a littl green."

Natalie controls the consistency of the paint mixture by carefully dipping the paintbrush in the water. When it is t runny, she pats the brush on the absorbent paper towel.

September 8 – 10:00 a.m.

Carla: "Look what happens when you dip the flower in the paint!"

Ana: "I think you made a discovery. How did you make that print?"

Carla: "I dipped it in the paint and gently put it on the paper."

Ana: "Can you show us how you created it?"

Carla repeats the process to demonstrate how she discovered her new painting technique.

September 8 – 12:45 p.m.

During the children's naptime, Ana invites other teachers to look at the children's collection of artwork and items that may be included in her developing documentation panel. Together, they discuss, reflect, and determine how they are going to arrange the final panel. Ana determines how it will be presented to communicate the "Sunflower Story."

Chapter 9

Expanding the Community of Support

You can't use up creativity. The more you use, the more you have.

—Maya Angelou, "Creativity: It's the Thought That Counts," interview with Mary Ardito for *Bell Telephone Magazine*

Children thrive on the support teachers give them every day in the classroom, but they also need a community that encourages their development, respects their ideas, and values them as individuals.

One of the challenges teachers face is how to involve families, guardians, and other significant people in children's lives in early childhood programs. Today's families are busy, with an abundance of obligations demanding their attention. With their resources already stretched so thin, some families are unwilling or unable to include extra commitments to their already heavy responsibilities. Therefore, it is necessary to be innovative as we think about ways to engage them in the program without producing additional stress on their already complicated lives.

The suggestions discussed in this chapter are just a few of the options that can be used to engage support from families and community members. Be flexible, and if one suggestion doesn't work, try a different approach. The goal is to build a robust community that encourages parents, guardians, and other adults to collaborate and search for innovative ways to nurture their children's creative development.

This budding artist is intensely focused on her drawing, adding details that she finds significant.

Engaging Families

Early childhood educators recognize that parents or guardians are their children's first teachers and that their contribution to their child's development is enormous. This understanding provides the foundation for a positive, reciprocal relationship between families and teachers as they work together to do what is best for children and create nurturing, stimulating environments both at home and at school. So how can you connect with families? What information can you share with each other? How can you collaborate to identify resources for children and families? What have parents experienced that they can share with other families?

Workshops for Families

One possibility is to come together for workshops that emphasize relationship building with families and children. Providing stimulating, hands-on workshops can help adults identify creative ideas, experience the creative thinking that their children need to develop, and recognize how to extend creative learning at home.

> **Thinking Outside the Box With Cardboard Building**
  Collect a wide assortment of cardboard boxes for adults to explore, build with, and combine with other materials you provide. During the work, you can pose questions: "What are you building?," "Would you like to add something new to your structure?," "How can you incorporate aluminum foil?," and "What can you build with these oddly shaped boxes?"

> **Paint a Wall: Setting Your Creative Spirit Free**
  Cover a large wall with white paper and provide a variety of painting tools—brushes, rollers, toothbrushes, spray bottles, cotton swabs, sponges—and tempera paint. Offer minimal to no instructions and just encourage the adults to explore the materials and be imaginative. As they work, comment on the positive benefits creative activities have for children (and adults!).

Encourage families to nurture their children's love of literacy by sharing books together.

> **Inspiring Stories: Reading Children's Books and Telling Stories**

Share and read books that parents and guardians can borrow from the classroom library to read at home with their children. Adults enjoy listening to these stories while learning the importance of children's language development. Encourage parents to record their own telling of a story or book, and keep these in your book area for children to listen to. If a story lends itself to being dramatized, adults can act out the plot and videotape their performance to share it. Encourage parents and guardians to also share stories with their children about their history, families, and their experiences growing up. These personal stories forge stronger family connections and build children's confidence and sense of community as they find themselves part of a larger support network.

> **Break Out the Band**

Singing and making and playing instruments involves collecting a wide assortment of items that can be combined and used to make sound. Parents can make simple rhythm instruments to take home and share with their children, including maracas (pebbles in a tin can), rhythm sticks (dowel rods and craft sticks), and harps (a shoebox and rubber bands). Actual instruments, such as keyboards, guitars, and microphones, can also be brought in for the activity. Select music that adults will enjoy and encourage a jam session where each person improvises playing an instrument of his choice in his own way.

> **Toy Hospital: Let's Work Together to Revive Tired Toys**

Collect battered and broken toys, games, and play materials from the classroom—or encourage families to bring items from home—for parents to help restore and repair by painting, sanding, and gluing. If a toy is beyond saving or parents see other possibilities when looking at them, they can be dismantled or reconstructed to create something new.

> **What Can We Make From That?**

Ask families to bring in inexpensive or recycled items from their homes, and host a toy-making workshop. You can also invite parents to bring toys, games, or books they have made and used with their children at home and share these ideas with each other.

> **Exploring Fantastic Centers: Making Choices and Playing With Ideas**

For this workshop, select three or four learning centers you have set up in your classroom. Explain to families how these centers work, what their children do in them, and what aspects most engage their children. Encourage families to pick a learning center to play, pretend, and interact in, and invite them to explore other centers in the classroom. Ask for their suggestions for other centers they think their children might enjoy.

> **Family Fun Night**
> This event is an opportunity for families and children to enjoy time together. Provide several tables with small blocks, puzzles, art materials, and well-loved books, and encourage everyone to explore the materials. Children will enjoy being the "teacher" as they show and explain to families how things work, what they like, and how to clean up when they are finished.

These workshop possibilities are participatory, engaging, and provide many learning opportunities for teachers and families. Through these workshops, teachers and families can share ideas for supporting creative efforts. As you create with them, offer comments and information about the learning that takes place when their children are involved in similar open-ended activities. Sharing this information while adults are engaged in creative activities is an effective way for them to learn and experience what thinking, problem solving, and persistence look and feel like for children. Tell positive stories about events in the classroom to express your interest in their children, build relationships, and provide ideas to apply at home. Ask parents to share creative pursuits they enjoy at home with their families. Always have handouts available for adults to take home with information relating to the workshop topic, additional ideas that are simple to implement, and suggestions of books and articles that cover the topic more extensively.

Grandparents and Senior Citizens

An enormous untapped resource for early childhood programs is the growing number of grandparents and seniors in our communities. Many are looking for opportunities to be engaged in their community and socially involved in meaningful experiences. Inviting seniors into early childhood programs to interact with children provides rewarding experiences for both children and seniors. Children who don't have grandparents living nearby benefit from older adults' warmth, responsiveness, and wisdom. Seniors enjoy interacting with energetic children filled with ideas and possibilities. Think about ways to involve senior citizens in meaningful experiences that will add new, valuable dimensions to your early childhood program.

Many grandparents and seniors in the community can be wonderful additions to your program. They can help a child having difficulty tying his shoelaces, share a favorite book with a small group, interact with children during lunch, or tell a story about their own childhood. During creative project times, they can collect materials, record children's comments about their work, and help arrange attractive displays. Their focused attention is rewarded with positive responses from both children and teachers.

Ways to Connect Seniors to Your Program

Senior citizens are a rich community resource for programs for children. They have valuable knowledge to contribute and a personal interest in communicating with children. There are many ways to for seniors and children to connect through enriching creativity opportunities.

Lunch With Grandparents

Invite each child's grandparents, foster grandparents, or older friends to share in a meal in your program. For children who live far away from their extend families, inviting seniors

Deal and Antonio's Story

On Deal's first visit to programs in Reggio Emilia, Italy, he feels privileged to admire firsthand the schools that provide such high-quality environments for children. As he tours one classroom, he observes an older man standing by a dilapidated bookcase and rummaging through a toolbox. When Deal asks the man—Antonio—about his building project, Antonio replies, "I am repairing this bookcase." Deal inquires, "Do you have a child or grandchild in the program?" Antonio smiles and answers, "I had a grandson here about 10 years ago, but not now. From time to time, I return to fix things." Deal is intrigued by Antonio's continued involvement in the program over such a long time, especially now that he has no child or grandchild in the program. He wonders how the Reggio Emilia program inspired such a personal commitment.

Reflection

In Reggio Emilia, there is a strong interest in the programs for children. Parents and the community are important to the programs; they share their talents, participate in planning, and contribute materials. People who no longer have children or grandchildren attending the school are also supportive. Antonio helped build bookcases when his grandson was attending the program, but even now—a decade later—when his grandson is grown, he is still committed to helping the teachers and children by providing his expertise in fixing things. His contribution is highly valued and he appreciates that the children still use the bookcases he made. Antonio's pride in helping the children and teachers brings him back year after year.

from the community at large will help every child feel included. Lunch can take place on a special day dedicated to grandparents or at more regular intervals throughout the year. Children will have the opportunity to create an invitation, play host, and hear stories from the seniors' childhoods. Spending time with and learning more about the seniors in their lives help children to expand their appreciation for them.

Informational Meeting With Seniors

Arrange meetings for seniors to learn about your program, the characteristics of children, and what learning looks like in your setting. Provide information and examples that help them see children as creative individuals with their own ideas. Remember that your program is different from the way things were when these seniors went to school. Help them recognize and understand these differences and call attention to any similarities as well as the need for creative thinkers in today's world. Let them know how valuable they will be in sharing their abilities, interests, and support. Follow up on the meeting by having individual children or the whole class make personal notes that communicate their appreciation for seniors' involvement and contributions to your program.

Create a Beautiful Display of Senior Helpers

Create an attractive display with photos of seniors interacting with the children. Include transcripts of conversations between children and seniors and any drawings the children make about these interactions. Other documentation that can be featured includes records of their contributions to creative projects or special talents they shared with the children. This visual representation will help volunteers see how important their involvement is to the children and teachers.

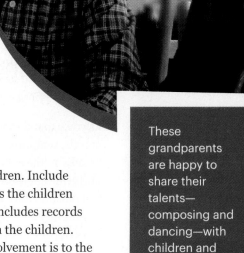

These grandparents are happy to share their talents— composing and dancing—with children and families.

Communication Tools: Connecting With Families

Newsletters. Newsletters, whether print or electronic, can be used to share information about the class (such as a new favorite song or updates on a long-term project), recap past events, or apprise families of upcoming events.

Websites and blogs. Many programs have a website that provides information about the program, introduces the staff, lists goals for learning, and announces creative workshops. A website can also include schedules, special dates, family requests, interesting projects, menus, and pictures of the children's work. Some teachers maintain blogs to keep families and interested people up to date with classroom activities, ongoing projects, and examples of children's imaginative thinking and learning.

Social media. Many teachers use social media to inform families about urgent needs, deadlines, or current happenings. On private networks, with families' permission, you might also include pictures and short videos of children participating in classroom activities.

Reading to and With a Child

Most children enjoy having stories read to them one-to-one. This personal reading time provides closeness for enjoying the book, discussing the content, and talking. Having seniors read or tell a story to a child is a special experience for both the child and adult. One senior, who read to a group of 3-year-olds on a weekly basis, shared with the program director, "This is the best part of my week!"

Other Suggestions for Senior Involvement

Take a survey of seniors' interests, talents, and anything else they might feel is worth contributing to the classroom. Here are just a few possibilities.

> **Cooking.** Have seniors share a favorite recipe and prepare it with a small group of children.

> **Cultivating a community garden.** Seniors who are experienced gardeners or who just want to participate in an outdoor activity can help children select and prepare a site for a class garden. Together, they and the children can decide what seeds to plant; water, weed, and maintain the garden; harvest the crops; and—best of all—eat what they grow together.

> **Sharing hobbies.** Seniors and children with similar personal interests can be partnered to explore a hobby together. Or perhaps a child can develop a new interest as they explore sewing, painting, writing, or singing with a senior.

> **Transcribing stories.** Children can dictate stories while seniors listen and write their words down. Seeing their words on a page helps children recognize the connection between oral language and printed text and view themselves as creative writers and storytellers. Once recorded, these stories can be reread and enjoyed many times.

Exhibiting Children's Work in the Community: Branching Out Locally

As you expand the creative opportunities available to children, you will be astonished by the murals, sculptures, writings, and creations they develop. These works should be shared more broadly in the community so others can enjoy the results and appreciate the importance of nurturing children's imaginations and creativity. Every community has venues where works and documentation of the creative process may be displayed for children, families, and community members to view and admire. Here are a few potential places to display children's work outside of the school setting.

Shopping Malls

Many towns have shopping malls close to schools or programs. Shopping centers usually have many empty walls that are perfect to display art. If the store management is willing to let your program use the space, arrange art shows to display the children's work—you might even collaborate with other local early childhood programs to coordinate a large exhibit. Displays will be seen by the children, parents, seniors, and anyone who lives and shops in the community. Your class's projects can make a big splash on formerly empty walls, and budding artists and inventors will feel proud to have their work publically displayed.

Art Galleries and Museums

Some art galleries and hands-on children's museums have space dedicated to exhibiting the work of children from local schools and early childhood programs. These respected, attractive settings give children an opportunity to see their work displayed in a professional setting with focused lighting and pedestals. Invite families to come appreciate the work; at the showing, children can describe their work and enjoy the recognition they receive.

Grocery Stores

A neighborhood grocery store may be transformed for a showing of your children's work. In addition to projects being accessible for children's families to enjoy, the audience will be greatly expanded to include anyone who shops in the grocery store. Display the children's works in frames and attractive groupings, and label each clearly with the name of the artist.

Local Restaurants or Cafés

Many communities have family-run restaurants or cafés where residents eat, work, or pass by on a daily basis. The windows and walls in these establishments provide additional spaces to spread the word that children are creative and that their efforts are worth appreciation.

Several 3-year-old children created this representation of a campfire using an original design and colors.

This colorful abstract painting was created by a group of children and displayed on a gallery wall for families and the community to admire.

Inviting Creative Visitors Into the Classroom

Artists, scientists, musicians, weavers, storytellers, dancers, and other creators are always a welcome addition to the early childhood classroom. Some children have never observed adult or professional creative thinkers at work. They would be enthralled to see a potter turn a blob of clay into a surprising sculpture before their eyes, listen to a musician improvise a familiar song, or join a dancer from Thailand in performing expressive choreography. Every community has people with skills and talents that children would enjoy observing in action. It might be one student's brother who plays the trombone in the high school band, a storyteller who creates original stories, or a weaver who turns yarn into hats. Bringing these guests into the classroom lets children observe and appreciate performers at work.

To facilitate creative development, provide children with opportunities to work alongside artists and other creative adults (Runco 2014; Sawyer 2012). In interviews with one hundred exceptional creators, Vera John-Steiner (1997) found that all of them had become immersed in their area of interest at an early age. Many early childhood programs do not have the resources to include an artist throughout the year. For these programs, a visiting or returning artist is a wonderful way to provide these experiences for young children. Artists can be found within your school or in those connected to your program. A parent with a background in photography may enjoy sharing her experiences and photographs with the children. A school administrator who plays Celtic melodies on his father's bagpipe may mesmerize and inspire children. Finding creative people within the community also provides a sense of richness, care, and respect for local artists. A neighbor, a former prima ballerina at the local ballet theater, could visit the classroom to show the children videos of some of her performances or the costumes she wore on stage. Each of these creative people will enrich and extend children's interest and insights by providing them with another connection to their community.

Before they come to your classroom, talk with visiting artists about some of the children's interests. Share that because the children are creative and very curious, they will want to touch and experience the tools or instruments the individual brings—and they will ask a lot of questions. Assure the visitor that you will be there to help if any assistance is needed.

Preparing Children for Visitors

Before any visitors arrive, it is important to share some initial information, pictures, and ideas with the children. Discuss how to respectfully observe, listen, and learn during this visit, and encourage children to come up with questions to ask. In addition, have them assist in any cleanup that might be necessary after a visit and impress on them the importance of thanking visitors for taking the time to share their talents with them.

Take pictures and record the children's words and responses during the visit. You can share a collection of these comments with visitors as a concrete way to show them the importance of their contribution to the program. Send a follow-up note sharing your thoughts about the experience and their involvement. Remember to express how valuable the experience of seeing an artist in action was for the children.

Thinking Big: Community Leaders, Elected Officials, and Governors

Venture out into the wide world filled with people who need to know about the inventiveness of children and recognize their learning capabilities. Spread the word throughout the community about the critical importance of the early years and the positive benefits of a high-quality early childhood program on children's development. To raise awareness, invite community and state leaders to visit your program so they can interact with the children and see the displays of their creative work in the classroom and community. A gallery exhibit or other special event could be the catalyst for community members to help you and families celebrate children.

Use the information and ideas discussed in this book to develop effective workshops and professional development opportunities and to share children's accomplishments with community leaders. Together, we can show that children are some of the most creative people in the world!

This visitor has a long history with this early childhood program. As a child, she attended one of the school's preschool programs and remembers her experiences clearly and fondly. Years later, she returns to volunteer and interact with the children in the same environment that was nurturing for her.

Reflections

> How might you involve senior citizens and parents in your classroom activities? How would this benefit children?

> Is there a local venue where you could display children's work? How could you exhibit their work so others can appreciate their imaginative nature?

> What artists, musicians, dancers, or storytellers can you invite to your classroom for the children to enjoy and appreciate their talents? Consider family members or seniors in addition to professionals. What follow-up activities could build on the materials and techniques used by these class visitors?

> How could you include leaders of the community in your program? What can you do to spread the word about the need for creative thinkers in the twenty-first century?

Evidence of Creating, Thinking, and Learning

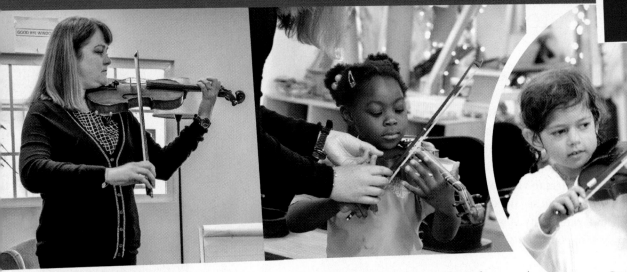

A violin teacher performs a variety of pieces for the children, including classical pieces, Irish jigs, and familiar children's songs.

Shari (age 4) explores the feel of the violin, the strings, and the bow. The violinist helps her hold the delicate instrument.

Ruth (age 4) attempts to play the violin independently.

Visual Art

This university art gallery announces a special showing of art collected and displayed as part of the exhibition *Through the Eyes of Children*.

This nest, cradling three papier-mâché eggs, is displayed on a raised pedestal.

This life-size mannequin has a plastic frame was built by the teachers. Several preschool decorated the figure by adding bottle lids, c sticks, twine, ribbons, fabric, coat hangers, thread, rings, and a beaded necklace.

Epilogue

Think left and think right and think low and think high. Oh, the thinks you can think up if only you try!

—Dr. Seuss, *Oh, the Thinks You Can Think!*

Creating a Tapestry

This book has outlined the reasons creativity is important for children in a rapidly changing world—to tackle critical issues, understand how to evaluate an ever-expanding knowledge base, adapt to evolving technology, develop the flexibility that the future workforce will need, and find meaning and joy in what they do. It is clear that thinkers and innovators are needed rather than copiers and repeaters of outdated information. Early childhood educators must nurture and support the innovators, creative thinkers, flexible adapters, communicators, and problem solvers in their classrooms to establish a "climate of creativity" (Runco 2014). Children will then be confident in their abilities to create, question, and act on their curiosity and adventurousness.

We are at a critical point in early childhood education where we must resist forces that are pushing for conformity, more testing, and less play. We must work to lessen the pressure to evaluate and compare young children based only on their academic skills while ignoring their strengths in other domains. Now is the time to nurture fundamental elements that children will need for the future—innovation, communication skills, collaboration, and critical thinking.

Developing environments and curriculum filled with creative learning opportunities across all learning domains is a complex and daunting task. As we create this intricate design—a tapestry—for learning, what are the components needed to sustain a creative mindset?

The Yarn: The Child

When looking back on their lives, creative geniuses (Big-C) often point to experiences from their early years of development as major influences on their creativity and accomplishments. Historical studies, current research, and experts on creativity have identified effective supports for nurturing children's creativity, including

> Valuing children's ideas

> Providing a variety of choices

> Offering a place to think and create

> Allowing children to follow their interests

> Designing a flexible environment that adapts to different needs

> Allowing children time to work at their own pace

> Providing the opportunity to revisit and refine their work

Children need an environment that supports their creativity, builds confidence in their growing creative capabilities, and encourages them to be imaginative risk takers. Teachers, parents, grandparents, and other members of the children's community can provide new insights, expand their experiences, and support the development of skills and knowledge they need to be successful.

"This is a pirate ship and the small shells are flags!"

The Weaver: The Teacher

You...

Are an essential part of a nurturing environment and an effective model for the children as you demonstrate creative thinking

Incorporate unique materials into the environment that reflect the children's interests and spark their creativity

Carefully balance guiding children's actions, facilitating their thinking, and giving them the freedom to move beyond your suggestions

Find joy in children's unusual suggestions and allow them to follow their ideas when working in centers, developing plays, displaying collections, exploring and experimenting with physical actions and reactions, and instigating projects

Value creative thinking, try new things, and support children when they are stuck or frustrated with their work

Pose productive (provocative) questions, actively listen to children's explanations, provide language to describe and accompany their experiences, respect their distinctive ideas, and adapt to their changing interests

Provide varied opportunities for collaboration (individual, partner, small group, and whole class)

Focus on setting up a classroom environment that activates children's thinking, provides the materials to support their innovations, and includes elements that will inspire and extend their possibilities

Believe that children are capable and creative

Are a careful observer of children's budding ideas

Provide positive support of children's early attempts and continued efforts and the framework for their innovative thinking and creative problem solving

Are vigilant in finding the strengths and passions of each child so they can be integrated into the classroom in ways that support their development

Recognize that children learn and create in many different ways and across all domains (literacy, math, science, technology, art, music and movement, and drama)

The Loom: The Environment

In an aesthetically pleasing classroom, there are many examples of children's creations, inventions, and experiments. It is a literacy-rich environment full of thoughtful conversations, stories, and project work. In this warm, light-filled space, materials are displayed, explored, and used to extend learning possibilities. Flexible, open-ended materials beckon children to unleash their imagination. There are areas arranged for different purposes, such as thinking quietly, exploring and investigating, solving problems, and working in small, collaborative groups.

The environment is conducive to experiences that enable children to practice and refine their social skills as they discover how to effectively work with others, influence their thinking, and respect their diverse ideas. There are also opportunities for children to define issues or problems, find solutions, and evaluate the effectiveness of their approaches. The classroom combines stable, familiar features with those that reflect new interests and growing capabilities.

Children, their diversity, and their families are visibly celebrated. There is joy and laughter as children play, explore, use symbols, take on roles, and find ways to collaborate. The children feel comfortable taking risks, doing things in different ways, and learning from their mistakes. This flexible thinking, coupled with novel experiences, provides a rich environment for inspiring and supporting innovative thinking. It provides encouragement for you and the children as you think, investigate materials, combine ideas, discard things that don't work, and return with renewed energy for future projects. This is the environment that will prepare children to live in the twenty-first century and face their future with confidence.

Together, the yarn (the child), the weaver (the teacher), and the loom (the environment) create a beautiful, original tapestry that combines children's ideas and teachers' thoughtful planning. Each element supports the miraculous possibilities that emerge, grow, develop, and transform.

Looking Ahead

Gladwell (2002) asserts that the field of early childhood is at a tipping point. Together, early childhood educators and families can spearhead a movement dedicated to appropriate learning for children that is holistic and includes creative thinking and the arts. This book and other resources will provide the tools and inspiration to support the development of young creative thinkers. With dedication and supportive information, we can be the voices that persuade the educational community to value, support, and implement practices that encourage the development of creativity in early childhood programs.

References

Adobe Systems. 2012. "State of Create Study: Global Benchmark Study on Attitudes and Beliefs About Creativity at Work, School, and Home." http://www.adobe.com/aboutadobe/pressroom/pdfs/Adobe _State_of_Create_Global_Benchmark_Study.pdf.

Amabile, T. M. 1983. *The Social Psychology of Creativity.* New York, NY: Springer-Verlag.

American Management Association (AMA). 2010. *AMA 2010 Critical Skills Survey: Executive Summary.* http://www.amanet.org/PDF/Critical-Skills-Survey.pdf.

Anderson, L.W., & D.R. Krathwohl, eds. 2001. *A Taxonomy for Learning, Teaching, and Assessing: A Revision of Bloom's Taxonomy of Educational Objectives.* New York, NY: Longman.

Applebee, A.N. 1978. *The Child's Concept of Story.* Chicago, IL: University of Chicago.

Bassok, D., S. Latham, & A. Rorem. 2016. "Is Kindergarten the New First Grade?" *AERA Open* 1 (4): 1–31. doi:10.1177/2332858415616358.

Batygin, K., & M. Brown. 2016. "Evidence for a distant giant planet in the solar system." *The Astronomical Journal* 151 (22): 1–12.

Bloom, B.S., ed. 1984. *Taxonomy of Educational Objectives: The Classification of Educational Goals.* White Plains, NY: Longman.

Bloomberg Business. "What Chief Executives Really Want." May 18, 2010. http://www.bloomberg.com/news /articles/2010-05-18/what-chief-executives-really-want.

Broadhead, P. 2004. *Early Years Play and Learning: Developing Social Skills and Cooperation.* London, UK: RoutledgeFalmer.

Bronson, P., & A. Merryman. "The Creativity Crisis." *Newsweek,* July 10, 2010. http://www.newsweek.com /creativity-crisis-74665.

Brown, S., & C. Vaughan. 2010. *Play: How It Shapes the Brain, Opens the Imagination, and Invigorates the Soul.* New York, NY: Avery.

Bruce, T. 2011. *Cultivating Creativity: For Babies, Toddlers and Young Children.* 2nd ed. London, UK: Hodder Education.

Carson, S. 2010. *Your Creative Brain: Seven Steps to Maximize Imagination, Productivity, and Innovation in Your Life.* San Francisco, CA: Jossey-Bass.

Chalufour, I., & K. Worth. 2004. *Building Structures with Young Children.* St. Paul, MN: Redleaf Press.

Craft, A. 2002. *Creativity and Early Years Education: A Lifewide Foundation.* London, UK: Continuum.

Csikszentmihalyi, M. 2009. *Flow: The Psychology of Optimal Experience.* New York, NY: Harper and Row.

Csikszentmihalyi, M. 2014. *Creativity: Flow and the Psychology of Discovery and Invention.* New York, NY: Harper Collins.

Daly, L., & M. Beloglovsky. 2015. *Loose Parts: Inspiring Play in Young Children.* St. Paul, MN: Redleaf Press.

Darling-Hammond, L., B. Barron, P.D. Pearson, A.H. Schoenfeld, E.K. Stage, T.D. Zimmerman, G.N. Cervetti, & J.L. Tilson. 2008. *Powerful Learning: What We Know About Teaching for Understanding.* San Francisco, CA: Jossey-Bass.

Dewey, J. 1915. *The School and Society.* Chicago, IL: University of Chicago Press.

Diamandis, P.H., & S. Kotler. 2012. *Abundance: The Future is Better Than You Think.* New York, NY: Free Press.

Edwards, C.P., & L. Gandini. 2015. "Teacher Research in Reggio Emilia: Essence of a Dynamic, Evolving Role." *Voices of Practitioners* 10 (Winter): 89–103. https://www.naeyc.org/files/naeyc/Teacher%20Research %20in%20Reggio%20Emilia.pdf.

Edwards, C.P., L. Gandini, & G. Forman, eds. 1998. *The Hundred Languages of Children: The Reggio Emilia Approach—Advanced Reflections*. 2nd ed. Greenwich, CT: Ablex Publishing.

Edwards, C.P., & K.W. Springate. 1995. *Encouraging Creativity in Early Childhood Classrooms* (ERIC Digest). Urbana, IL: ERIC Clearinghouse on Elementary and Early Childhood Education. (ED389474).

Edwards, L.C. 2010. *The Creative Arts: A Process Approach for Teachers and Children*. 5th ed. Upper Saddle River, NJ: Merrill.

Elstgeest, J. 2001. "The Right Question at the Right Time." In *Primary Science: Taking the Plunge*, 2nd ed., ed. W. Harlen, 25–35. Portsmouth, NH: Heinemann.

Epstein, A.S. 2014. *The Intentional Teacher: Choosing the Best Strategies for Young Children's Learning*. Rev. ed. Washington, DC: NAEYC.

Erickson, E.H. 1980. *Identity and the Life Cycle*. New York, NY: W.W. Norton & Company.

Esquivel, G.B. 1995. "Teacher Behaviors that Foster Creativity." *Educational Psychology Review* 7 (2): 185–202.

Feldman, D. 1980. *Beyond Universals in Cognitive Development*. Norwood, NJ: Ablex Publishing.

Florida, R.L. 2004. "America's Looming Creativity Crisis." *Harvard Business Review* 82 (10): 122–136. doi: 10.1225/R0410H.

Florida, R.L. 2012. *The Rise of the Creative Class: And How It's Transforming Work, Leisure, Community, and Everyday Life*. New York, NY: Basic Books.

Fowlkes, M.A. 1992. "Patty Smith Hill: Pivotal Figure in Childhood Education." Paper presented at the Association for Childhood Education International, in New York, NY, October.

Fox, J.E., & R. Schirrmacher. 2015. *Art and Creative Development for Young Children*. 8th ed. Belmont, CA: Wadsworth Cengage Learning.

Fröebel, F. [1826] 2005. *The Education of Man*. Trans. W.N. Hailmann. Mineola, NY: Dover Publications.

Fusco, E. 2012. *Effective Questioning Strategies in the Classroom: A Step-by-Step Approach to Engaged Thinking and Learning, K–8*. New York, NY: Teachers College Press.

Gandini, L. 2005. *In the Spirit of the Studio: Learning from the Atelier of Reggio Emilia*. New York, NY: Teachers College Press.

Gandini, L., & J. Goldhaber. 2001. "Two Reflections About Documentation." In *Bambini: The Italian Approach to Infant/Toddler Care*, eds. L. Gandini & C.P. Edwards, 124–145. New York, NY: Teachers College Press.

Gardner, H. 2011. *Frames of Mind: The Theory of Multiple Intelligences*. New York, NY: Basic Books.

Gazzaniga, M.S., & R.W. Sperry. 1967. "Language After Section of the Cerebral Commissures." *Brain* 90 (1): 131–148.

Given, H., L. Kuh, D. LeeKeenan, B. Mardell, S. Redditt, & S. Twombly. 2010. "Changing School Culture: Using Documentation to Support Collaborative Inquiry." *Theory Into Practice* 49 (1): 36–46. doi: 10.1080/00405840903435733.

Gladwell, M. 2002. *The Tipping Point: How Little Things Can Make a Big Difference*. Boston, MA: Back Bay.

Goldstein, E.B. 2014. *Sensation and Perception*. 9th ed. Belmont, CA: Wadsworth.

GOV.UK. 2016. "Early Years Foundation Phase." Last modified March 24. https://www.gov.uk/early-years-foundation-stage.

Guilford, J.P. 1967. *The Nature of Human Intelligence*. New York, NY: McGraw-Hill.

Hawkins, D. 2002. *The Informed Vision: Essays on Learning and Human Nature*. New York, NY: Algora Publishing.

Helm, J.H., & L.G. Katz. 2011. *Young Investigators: The Project Approach in the Early Years*. 2nd ed. New York, NY: Teachers College Press.

Hildebrandt, C. 1998. "Creativity in Music and Early Childhood." *Young Children* 53 (6): 68–74.

Hildebrandt, C. & B. Zan. 2002. "Exploring the Art and Science of Musical Sound." In *Developing Constructivist Early Childhood Curriculum: Practical Principles and Activities,* eds, R. DeVries, B. Zan, C. Hildebrandt, R. Edmiaston, & C. Sales, 101–120. New York, NY: Teachers College Press.

Hill, L.A., G. Brandeau, E. Truelove, & K. Lineback. 2014. *Collective Genius: The Art and Practice of Leading Innovation.* Boston, MA: Harvard Business Review.

Hirsh-Pasek, K., R.M. Golinkoff, L.E. Berk, & D.G. Singer. 2009. *A Mandate for Playful Learning in Preschool: Presenting the Evidence.* New York, NY: Oxford University Press.

Hiskey, D. "Post-It Notes Were Invented By Accident." *Today I Found Out: Feed Your Brain,* November 9, 2011. http://www.todayifoundout.com/index.php/2011/11/post-it-notes-were-invented-by-accident.

Hui, A.N.N., M.W.-J. He, & E.S.C. Liu. 2013. "Creativity and Early Talent Development in the Arts in Young and Schoolchildren." In *Creativity, Talent, and Excellence,* ed. A.-G. Tan, 75-87. New York, NY: Springer.

Isaksen, S.G. 1987. "A New Dimension for Creativity Research: Examining Style and Level of Creativity." Paper presented at the Kirton Adaptor-Innovator Conference, in Hertfordshire, UK, July.

Isbell, C., & R.T. Isbell. 2008. *Sensory Integration: A Guide for Preschool Teachers.* Beltsville, MD: Gryphon House.

Isbell, R.T., & P. Evanshen. 2012. *Real Classroom Makeovers: Practical Ideas for Early Childhood Classrooms.* Lewisville, NC: Gryphon House.

Isbell, R.T., & S.C. Raines. 2013. *Creativity and the Arts with Young Children.* 3rd ed. Belmont, CA: Wadsworth.

Isenberg, J.P., & J.L. Durham. 2015. *Creative Materials and Activities for the Early Childhood Curriculum.* Hoboken, NJ: Pearson.

Isenberg, J.P., & M.R. Jalongo. 2014. *Creative Thinking and Arts-Based Learning: Preschool Through Fourth Grade.* 6th ed. Boston, MA: Pearson.

Jervis, K., & A. Tobier, eds. 1988. *Education for Democracy: Proceedings from the Cambridge School Conference on Progressive Education, October, 1987.* Weston, MA: Cambridge.

John-Steiner, V. 1997. *Notebooks of the Mind: Explorations of Thinking.* New York, NY: Oxford University Press.

Johnson, K. "Pluto Gets New Name, as Does 'Xena.'" *National Geographic News,* September 15, 2006. http://news.nationalgeographic.com/news/2006/09/060915-pluto-name.html.

Katz, L.G., & S.C. Chard. 1999. *Engaging Children's Minds: The Project Approach.* Norwood, NJ: Ablex Publishing.

Kaufman, J.C., & R.A. Beghetto. 2009. "Beyond Big and Little: The Four C Model of Creativity." *Review of General Psychology* 13 (1): 1–12. doi:10.1037/a0013688.

Kelley, L., & B. Sutton-Smith. 1987. "A Study of Infant Musical Productivity." In *Music and Child Development,* eds. J.C. Peery, I.W. Peery, & T.W. Draper, 35–53. New York, NY: Springer-Verlag. doi:10.1007/978-1-4613-8698-8.

Kelley, T., & D. Kelley. 2013. *Creative Confidence: Unleashing the Creative Potential Within Us All.* New York, NY: Crown Business.

Kelley, T., & J. Littman. 2002. *The Art of Innovation: Lessons in Creativity from IDEO, America's Leading Design Firm.* London, UK: Harper Collins Business.

Kim, K.H. 2011. "The Creativity Crisis: The Decrease in Creative Thinking Scores on the Torrance Tests of Creative Thinking." *Creativity Research Journal* 23 (4): 285–295. doi:10.1080/10400419.2011.627805.

Kohlberg, L. 1984. *The Psychology of Moral Development: The Nature and Validity of Moral Stages.* Vol. 2, *Essays on Moral Development.* San Francisco, CA: Harper & Row.

Korn-Bursztyn, C., ed. 2012. *Young Children and the Arts: Nurturing Imagination and Creativity.* Charlotte, NC: Information Age.

Lascarides, V.C., & B.F. Hinitz. 2000. *History of Early Childhood Education*. New York, NY: Routledge.

Lehrer, J. 2012. *Imagine: How Creativity Works*. Boston, MA: Houghton Mifflin Harcourt.

Martens, M.L. 1999. "Productive Questions: Tools for Supporting Constructivist Learning." *Science and Children* 36 (8): 24–27, 53.

Metla, V. "School Art Programs: Should They Be Saved?: *Law Street,* May 14, 2015. http://lawstreetmedia .com/issues/education/cutting-art-programs-schools-solution-part-problem.

Mihov, K.M., M. Denzler, & J. Förster. 2010. "Hemispheric Specialization and Creative Thinking: A Meta-Analytic Review of Lateralization of Creativity." *Brain and Cognition* 72 (3): 442–448. doi:10.1016/j .bandc.2009.12.007.

Milteer, R.M., & K.R. Ginsburg. 2012. "The Importance of Play in Promoting Healthy Child Development and Maintaining Strong Parent-Child Bonds: Focus on Children in Poverty." *Pediatrics* 129 (1): e204–e213. doi:10.1542/peds.2011-2953.

Naisbitt, J. 1982. *Megatrends: Ten New Directions Transforming Our Lives*. New York, NY: Warner Books.

National Association for Music Education (NAfME). 2016. "Early Childhood Education." Position Statement. Reston, VA: NAfMA. http://www.nafme.org/about/position-statements/early-childhood-education -position-statement/early-childhood-education.

National Center for Families Learning (NCFL). 2015. "Wonder of the Day #473: Who Invented Sticky Notes?" Wonderopolis. Accessed June 22. http://wonderopolis.org/wonder/who-invented-sticky-notes.

National Education Association (NEA). 2011. "Preparing 21st Century Students for a Global Society: An Educator's Guide to the 'Four Cs.'" http://www.nea.org/assets/docs/A-Guide-to-Four-Cs.pdf.

Nicholson, S. 1972. "The Theory of Loose Parts: An Important Principle for Design Methodology." *Studies in Design Education Craft & Technology* 4 (2): 5–14.

Pellegrini, A. D., & K. Gustafson. 2005. "Boys' and Girls' Uses of Objects for Exploration, Play, and Tools in Early Childhood." In *The Nature of Play: Great Apes and Humans,* eds. A.D. Pellegrini & P.K. Smith, 113–138. New York, NY: Guilford.

Piaget, J. 1954. *The Construction of Reality in the Child*. New York, NY: Basic Books.

Piaget, J. 1971. *Biology and Knowledge: An Essay on the Relations Between Organic Regulations and Cognitive Processes*. Chicago, IL: University of Chicago.

Piaget, J., & B. Inhelder. 1969. *The Psychology of the Child*. New York, NY: Basic Books.

Pica, R. 2013. *Experiences in Movement and Music: Birth to Age Eight*. 5th ed. Belmont, CA: Wadsworth Cengage.

Pink, D.H. 2006. *A Whole New Mind: Why Right-Brainers Will Rule the Future*. New York, NY: Riverhead Books.

Posner, M.I., & B. Patoine. "How Arts Training Improves Attention and Cognition." *The Dana Foundation*, September 14, 2009. http://dana.org/Cerebrum/2009/How_Arts_Training_Improves_Attention_and _Cognition.

Rauscher, F.H., G.L. Shaw, L.J. Levine, E.L. Wright, W.R. Dennis, & R.L. Newcomb. 1997. "Music Training Causes Long-term Enhancement of Preschool Children's Spatial-Temporal Reasoning." *Neurological Research* 19 (1): 2–8.

Renzulli, J.S., & C.F. De Wet. 2010. "Developing Creative Productivity in Young People Through the Pursuit of Ideal Acts of Learning. In *Nurturing Creativity in the Classroom,* eds. R.A. Beghetto & J. C. Kaufman, 24–72. New York, NY: Cambridge University Press.

Resnick, M. 2007. "All I Really Need to Know (About Creative Thinking) I Learned (By Studying How Children Learn) in Kindergarten." *Proceedings of the 6th ACM SIGCHI Conference on Creativity & Cognition*, 1–6. doi:10.1145/1254960.1254961.

Ritchhart, R., M. Church, & K. Morrison. 2011. *Making Thinking Visible: How to Promote Engagement, Understanding, and Independence for All Learners*. San Francisco, CA: Jossey-Bass.

Runco, M.A. 2014. *Creativity: Theories and Themes: Research, Development, and Practice.* 2nd ed. London, UK: Elsevier.

Sarama, J., & D.H. Clements. 2004. "Building Blocks for Early Childhood Mathematics." *Early Childhood Research Quarterly* 19 (1): 181–189. doi:10.1016/j.ecresq.2004.01.014.

Sarama, J., & D.H. Clements. 2009. "Building Blocks and Cognitive Building Blocks: Playing to Know the World Mathematically." *American Journal of Play* 1 (3): 313–337. http://www.journalofplay.org/sites/www.journalofplay.org/files/pdf-articles/1-3-article-building-blocks-cognitive-building-blocks.pdf.

Sawyer, R.K. 2012. *Explaining Creativity: The Science of Human Innovation.* 2nd ed. New York, NY: Oxford Press.

Sawyer, R.K. 2013. *Zig Zag: The Surprising Path to Constant Creativity.* San Francisco, CA: Jossey-Bass.

Sharp, C. 2004. "Developing Young Children's Creativity: What Can We Learn from Research?" *Topic* 32: 5–12. Retrieved from http://www.nfer.ac.uk/nfer/publications/55502/55502.pdf.

Sluss, D.J. & O.S. Jarrett, eds. 2007. *Investigating Play in the 21st Century.* Vol. 7, *Play & Culture Studies.* Lanham, MD: University Press of America.

Smilansky, S., & L. Shefatya. 1990. *Facilitating Play: A Medium for Promoting Cognitive, Socio-Emotional, and Academic Development in Young Children.* Gaithersburg, MD: Psychosocial & Educational Publications.

Smolen, W. 2015. "The Sandbox Summit Story." Sandbox Summit. Accessed June 1. http://sandboxsummit.org/about (site discontinued).

Starko, A.J. 2014. *Creativity in the Classroom: Schools of Curious Delight.* 5th ed. New York, NY: Routledge.

Strasburger, V.C., B.J. Wilson, & A.B. Jordan. 2014. *Children, Adolescents, and the Media.* 3rd ed. Thousand Oaks, CA: Sage.

Tegano, D.W., M.M. Groves, & C.E. Catron. 1999. "Early Childhood Teachers' Playfulness and Ambiguity Tolerance: Essential Elements of Encouraging Creative Potential of Children." *Journal of Early Childhood Teacher Education* 20 (3): 291–300. doi:10.1080/0163638990200307.

Tegano, D.W., J.D. Moran III, & J.K. Sawyers. 1991. *Creativity in Early Childhood Classrooms.* Washington, DC: National Education Association. http://files.eric.ed.gov/fulltext/ED3384 35.pdf.

Thompson, S., J.G. Greer, & B.B. Greer. 2004. "Highly Qualified for Successful Teaching: Characteristics Every Teacher Should Possess." *Essays in Education* 10 (Summer).

Topal, C.W., & L. Gandini. 1999. *Beautiful Stuff! Learning with Found Materials.* Worcester, MA: Davis Publications.

Torrance, E.P. 1962. *Guiding Creative Talent.* Englewood Cliffs, NJ: Prentice-Hall.

Torrance, E.P. 1965. *Rewarding Creative Behavior: Experiments in Classroom Activity.* Englewood Cliffs, NJ: Prentice-Hall.

Trilling, B., & C. Fadel. 2009. *21st Century Skills: Learning for Life in Our Times.* San Francisco, CA: Jossey-Bass.

Vartanian, O., A.S. Bristol, & J.C. Kaufman, eds. 2013. *Neuroscience of Creativity.* Cambridge, MA: MIT Press.

Vong, K.-L. 2008. *Evolving Creativity: New Pedagogies for Young Children in China.* Staffordshire, UK: Trentham Books.

Vygotsky, L.S. 1930. "Imagination and Creativity in Childhood." *Journal of Russian and East European Psychology* 28 (1): 84–96.

Vygotsky, L.S. [1930–35] 1978. *Mind in Society: The Development of Higher Psychological Processes.* Ed. and trans. M. Cole, V. John-Steiner, S. Scribner, & E. Souberman. Cambridge, MA: Harvard University Press.

Wallas, G. 1926. *The Art of Thought.* New York, NY: Harcourt.

Ward, T.B., & K.N. Saunders. 2003. "Creativity." In Vol. 1 of *Encyclopedia of Cognitive Science,* ed. L. Nadel. London, UK: Nature Publishing Group.

Welsh Government. 2015. "Foundation Phase: The Statutory Curriculum for All 3- to 7-year-olds in Wales, in Both Maintained and Non-Maintained Settings." Last modified August 3. http://gov.wales/topics /educationandskills/earlyyearshome/foundation-phase/?lang=en.

Whitebread, D. 2012. *The Importance of Play: A Report on the Value of Children's Play with a Series of Policy Recommendations.* Toy Industries of Europe. http://www.importanceofplay.eu/IMG/pdf/dr_david _whitebread_-_the_importance_of_play.pdf.

Wolfe, J. 2000. *Learning from the Past: Historical Voices in Early Childhood Education.* Mayerthorpe, AB, Canada: Piney Branch Press.

Zane, L.M. 2015. *Pedagogy and Space: Design Inspirations for Early Childhood Classrooms.* St. Paul, MN: Redleaf Press.

Zigler, E., & J. Valentine. 1979. *Project Head Start: A Legacy of the War on Poverty.* New York, NY: Free Press.

About the Authors

Rebecca Isbell, PhD, is an early childhood consultant and professor emerita at East Tennessee State University, where she received the Distinguished Faculty Award in Teaching. She is former director of the Center of Excellence in Early Childhood Learning and Development at the university. She is the author of 12 books, including *Creativity and the Arts for Young Children,* 3rd ed., a textbook widely used in early childhood classes. Her early childhood experiences include directing a laboratory school (serving infants through kindergarten), teaching music, teaching children from toddler age through third grade, and coordinating a program for gifted and talented children.

Rebecca was raised in a musical family and a home filled with stories told by her father. She sang her first solo in church at age 4, and has continued to sing in choruses and with madrigal singers and to participate in dramatic productions. Recently she recorded her first CD filled with traditional songs for young children, *Songs Too Good to Miss.* Her first grade teacher asked her to tell a story to her classmates, and Rebecca has been telling stories to children, students, and adults ever since. She lives in Jonesborough, Tennessee, the home of the National Storytelling Festival. Today, Rebecca presents keynotes and sessions that celebrate creative children and are filled with music, stories, and laughter.

Sonia Akiko Yoshizawa is a PhD fellow in early childhood education at East Tennessee State University. She formerly served as a research associate at the Regents' Center for Early Developmental Education and the Center for Early Education in Science, Technology, Engineering, and Mathematics, both at the University of Northern Iowa. She coauthored a chapter in *STEM Learning with Young Children: Inquiry Teaching with Ramps and Pathways,* addressing how teachers can implement constructivist, research-based physical science activities.

Born in Japan and raised in São Paulo, Brazil, Sonia had artistic parents who played a significant role in her life, creating an environment filled with art, music, dance, and people of diverse backgrounds and abilities. Sonia's initial dream was to become a concert pianist. When she returned to Japan, she began a career in early childhood as a teacher, music instructor, and a director at the American Embassy School. She cofounded Tokyo Association of International Preschools. In the United States, Sonia continues to learn and to inspire teachers by conducting professional development and presentations. She is a co-facilitator of the Early Childhood Science Interest Forum for NAEYC.

Acknowledgments

Many people contributed to filling this book with ideas, possibilities, tales of inspiring teachers and creative children, documentation of projects, and captivating photographs. We are grateful to each one.

During this entire process, we worked with an amazing "think tank" composed of creative educators Dr. Angie Baker, Mary Myron, and Joy Matson and occupational therapist Jill Smith. Often, such think tanks include people outside of a particular field because they provide a different perspective on problems and identify unique solutions. This wonderful group brainstormed, discussed, and collaborated to guide the development of this book, including identifying topics that should be addressed, potential questions readers might have, and suggestions to inspire children's creative pursuits. Their experiences and ideas helped shape this book so that it would resonate with early childhood educators.

We believe that the photographs of children and teachers engaging in creative endeavors are a special feature of this book. Sonia Yoshizawa and Edwel Granadozo spent long hours in early childhood programs capturing images of children engaged in creative thinking. Their professional expertise is evident in the photographs throughout this book, many of which show not just the "aha!" moment children experienced but also the steps in the creative process.

We are blessed to have a high-quality, Reggio-inspired laboratory school on our university campus. This program, led by Beverly Wiginton, has a dedicated group of master teachers, child care specialists, and student assistants who welcomed us into their classrooms, let us stay for extensive periods of time, and sometimes rearranged the environment to help us get the best photograph opportunities. These teachers include Darrellen Lodien, Stephanie Stephens, Joy Matson, Gloria Reilly, Jackie Vaughn, Ann Marie Cornelison, Deb Oglesby, Kathy Carter-Bullen, Randa Dunlap, Amber Vaughn, and Joshua Cox, as well as volunteer Heather Harlan. The marvelous examples of creative projects, unique work, and innovative possibilities happened in their classrooms and with their inspiration.

We are also grateful to the other programs reflected in the book's examples and photographs. At the Tennessee State Voluntary Pre-K program in Unicoi County, Jenifer Lingerfelt was the director and contributed photographs from her classrooms. This model program is a wonderful example of a state program for young children that positively impacts their lives today and in the future.

At Miller Perry Elementary School in Sullivan County, Tennessee, principal Angie Baker is a specialist in early childhood education and acutely aware of children's enormous capacity for creativity. For this book, she collaborated with the art teacher and kindergarten teachers in her program to involve children in constructing three-dimensional projects.

The kindergarten classroom at East Tennessee State University School served as another site to document young children's involvement in creative experiences, guided by inspiring teacher Mary Myron.

A number of families allowed us to observe, photograph, and record their children's activities. The parents at East Tennessee State University's Child Study Center, the University School kindergarten, and the Unicoi program recognized the importance of providing evidence of their children's creativity and learning. Lucas and Manuela Camargo-Carrillo and Christian and Hillary Schmid helped us photograph their children's investigations of shells, rocks, and clay.

Our early drafts of this book were reviewed by Dr. Sheila Smith, who provided the detailed analysis that clarified our work. Dr. Ruth Granadozo contributed her special skills transcribing children's conversations, and Laura Harrington, a visiting violinist, encouraged the children to explore string instruments and interacted with them in very supportive ways.

Our outstanding NAEYC editors, Kathy Charner, Holly Bohart, and Rossella Procopio, helped refine our words, caught our oversights, and supported our efforts throughout the birthing process. Lindsay Dirienzo and the NAEYC Creative Services team produced a magical artistic layout for the book. Thank you for hanging in there with us through this long journey.

It is our hope that this book will nurture your own creativity, and that you will inspire the creativity of all the children you work with each day!